"BIST has made a tremendous impact on our school culture. The BIST practices and common language among students, teachers, and staff provide the foundation for continuous growth and ownership of behaviors. After utilizing BIST to transform a large urban high school, we brought it to our rural school unit district to implement as part of our continuous culture shift. BIST is not a program but a piece of our overall foundation of Pride and Excellence."

Brett M. Elliott, *Superintendent of Stark County CUSD #100, IL*

"Young people need consistent support from adults in their lives. BIST is a proven solution that equips adults with the knowledge and skills needed to support young people in any setting, whether that be in a school, foster home, or in the community. Whether you're a parent, teacher, or school principal, Marty Huitt and Gail Tolbert will not only motivate you, but provide you with practical and usable skills to support young people in being healthy, safe, and successful in all aspects of their lives. Marty's humor, especially, is only matched by her spirit, care, and knowledge. She brings all of this together with her decades of teaching and training to inspire educators and other caregivers to be their best in supporting young people from classrooms to living rooms across the United States."

Ryan R. Dowis, *Executive Director of Family Focused Treatment Association, NJ*

"Over the past sixteen years, with the implementation of the BIST philosophy, I have seen schools increase their consistency of care for students in order to create greater levels of success for both children and adults. When schools embrace BIST, I see many teachers rediscover their passion for teaching."

Judith Soltys, *BIST Manager/Consultant, Kansas City, MO*

Cultivating Behavioral Change in K–12 Students

Cultivating Behavioral Change in K–12 Students provides in-service educators with a long-term, team-based approach to enhancing their interventions and supports for struggling students. Given the clear visibility of trauma, crisis, and clinical challenges among children today, it is more important than ever that school professionals have the tools to create a more consistent culture of care at their schools. This book is driven by tried-and-true strategies refined across the three decades of implementation of the Behavior Intervention Support Team (BIST) Model. Comprehensive and compassionate, these evidence-based practices target the sustainable transformation of young learners' behavior and help to shift the mindsets of the adults working with them. Principals, administrators, mental health practitioners, and teacher-leaders will be better prepared and motivated to collaborate toward student behavioral change, foster productive relationships with children and families, encourage learners to hone skills specific to behavior management, and more.

Marty Huitt is Director of the Behavior Intervention Support Team (BIST) at Cornerstones of Care, a trauma-informed behavioral healthcare nonprofit that partners with communities to improve the safety and health of children and families in Kansas, Missouri, and beyond. A former teacher, Marty has led the BIST team since 2003 and has worked with schools across the Midwest to create sustainable change for children.

Gail Tolbert, a former principal and teacher, is an educational consultant who specializes in school improvement. She has worked with the BIST team since 2013.

Also Available from Routledge Eye on Education
(www.routledge.com/k-12)

Educators as First Responders: A Teacher's Guide to Adolescent Development and Mental Health, Grades 6-12
Deborah Offner

Learner Choice, Learner Voice: A Teacher's Guide to Promoting Agency in the Classroom
Ryan L Schaaf, Becky Zayas, Ian Jukes

Supporting Student Mental Health: Essentials for Teachers
Michael Hass, Amy Ardell

The K-12 Educator's Data Guidebook: Reimagining Practical Data Use in Schools
Ryan A. Estrellado

The Brain-Based Classroom: Accessing Every Child's Potential Through Educational Neuroscience
Kieran O'Mahony

The Media-Savvy Middle School Classroom: Strategies for Teaching Against Disinformation
Susan Brooks-Young

Cultivating Behavioral Change in K–12 Students

Team-Based Intervention and Support Strategies

Marty Huitt
with Gail Tolbert

Taylor & Francis Group
NEW YORK AND LONDON

Designed cover image: © Shutterstock

First published 2024
by Routledge
605 Third Avenue, New York, NY 10158

and by Routledge
4 Park Square, Milton Park, Abingdon, Oxon, OX14 4RN

Routledge is an imprint of the Taylor & Francis Group, an informa business

© 2024 Marty Huitt with Gail Tolbert

The right of Marty Huitt with Gail Tolbert, to be identified as authors of this work has been asserted in accordance with sections 77 and 78 of the Copyright, Designs and Patents Act 1988.

All rights reserved. No part of this book may be reprinted or reproduced or utilised in any form or by any electronic, mechanical, or other means, now known or hereafter invented, including photocopying and recording, or in any information storage or retrieval system, without permission in writing from the publishers.

Trademark notice: Product or corporate names may be trademarks or registered trademarks, and are used only for identification and explanation without intent to infringe.

Library of Congress Cataloging-in-Publication Data
Names: Huitt, Marty, author. | Tolbert, Gail, author.
Title: Cultivating behavioral change in K-12 students : team-based intervention and support strategies / Marty Huitt, with Gail Tolbert.
Description: First edition. | New York : Routledge, 2024. | Includes bibliographical references and index.
Identifiers: LCCN 2023041486 (print) | LCCN 2023041487 (ebook) | ISBN 9781032586335 (hbk) | ISBN 9781032620466 (pbk) | ISBN 9781032620480 (ebk)
Subjects: LCSH: School psychology--United States. | Behavior modification--United States. | School children--United States--Discipline. | Classroom management--United States. | School improvement programs--United States. | Teachers--Social networks.
Classification: LCC LB1027.55 .H85 2024 (print) | LCC LB1027.55 (ebook) | DDC 370.150973--dc23/eng/20231121
LC record available at https://lccn.loc.gov/2023041486
LC ebook record available at https://lccn.loc.gov/2023041487

ISBN: 978-1-032-58633-5 (hbk)
ISBN: 978-1-032-62046-6 (pbk)
ISBN: 978-1-032-62048-0 (ebk)

DOI: 10.4324/9781032620480

Typeset in Optima
by SPi Technologies India Pvt Ltd (Straive)

For Harold and Dorothy Huitt

Growing up in a Midwestern, rural community, our family was constantly living on the poverty line. My father was a minister, and my mother did not work outside of the home due to raising seven children. As a child I had the experience of witnessing my parents incredible work ethic and their constant compassion for people. Several years ago, as my father was dying, I promised him that I would continue his work by delivering the message of compassion and care for all.

Contents

Preface	xi
Introduction	1
1 "I Can't Help All of These Kids." Of Course You Can!	3
History of BIST	5
Why Are There So Many Behavior Problems?	6
The Foundation of BIST	10
2 Now What?	23
Clarity on Common Area Expectations	25
Classroom Management	26
Consistency	30
Providing What Students Need	32
Intentionally Supporting Change	42
3 BIST Logistics	72
BIST Continuum of Logistics	72
Processing	78
Team Focus (Long-Term Recovery Process)	81
Suspension Re-entry Process	85
Prevention	86
4 "Our Kids" Community	112
Creating Cohesiveness in the Community by Avoiding Polarization	113
Clarifying Management of Behavior	115
Intentional Messaging with Colleagues	116
The Journey of Being an "Our Kids" Community	119

5	**Increasing Partnerships with Families**	**123**
	Communicating with Families	124
	Communicating Difficult Information	127
	Parent–Teacher Conferences	128
6	**Enhancing Our Vision, Growing Our Impact**	**132**
	Why Do You Need a Vision for the Culture Regarding Behavior?	133
	What Is Your Vision for Student Behavior and the Culture That Cultivates It?	134
	How Do You Share Your Vision?	137
	How Do You Inspire and Motivate People to Participate in Your Vision?	139
	How Do You Hold Teachers Accountable to Your Vision?	140
	Rubric for Adult Accountability	150
7	**Capacity: Increasing Ownership**	**153**
	Creating Capacity to Ensure the Vision	154
	Creating the Tipping Point	157
	Sustainability	158

Preface

There is an ever-growing need for schools to develop and practice a balanced approach when working with students that struggle behaviorally. To make this approach impactful, educators must change their mindset about what children need to achieve success. This shift in thinking and the opportunity it provides is the motivation for this book. Ideally, this can become not just an individual effort, but rather a community endeavor.

I started working with the Behavior Intervention Support Team (BIST) in 1997 after spending time in the classroom as a teacher of emotionally disturbed children both in public schools and in a residential setting. Before leaving the classroom, I had the opportunity to utilize the BIST Model. While practicing these concepts, I saw a positive impact on student behavior. Also, not only did I experience personal growth, I saw the adults in my school community begin to think about children that struggle in a very different manner. In this journey, the adults felt greater amounts of efficacy in their ability to support students not only academically but also behaviorally in a way that could be implemented in and sustained beyond the classroom.

Since joining the BIST Team in 1997, the work of supporting staff and students has continued to grow. I became the director in 2003 and over the course of those years, I have witnessed incredible work from both individuals in education as well as entire school communities. As schools evolve in their endeavor to better meet the needs of students, what has not changed is what children need emotionally – Grace and Accountability. This book is an attempt to articulate the foundational beliefs needed to increase success within our school systems. Grace is the unconditional relationship that students need. Accountability is the kind, guidance through ownership,

Preface

partnership and coachability. Both are needed in order to ensure future success and sustainability.

Since 1990, the BIST Team has provided training, support for implementation, as well as classroom resources. However, there has never been a comprehensive compilation of the concepts as well as the practices that make this model successful. Throughout this book the concepts of Grace and Accountability are prevalent; however, the practical strategies to put this thinking into play are the bulk of the content. While reading this information, the goal is to inspire hope that children who struggle are not only worthy of success but as adults we can help them achieve that success.

Marty Huitt
Kansas City
August 2023

I spent 35 years in public education as a teacher, administrator, and consultant. I have known Marty for 15 of those years and knew she had a great book in her. She not only talks about supporting adults and children with Grace and Accountability, but she lives it on a daily basis. I told her that I would help her write her book. This is the information I needed when I was a teacher and principal. It has been an honor to work with Marty.

Gail Tolbert
Kansas City
August 2023

Introduction

Our school was weary. Students' overwhelming emotional and behavioral needs were at an all-time high. Teachers felt under-supported and isolated, while administrators and counselors struggled to meet the ever-growing demands of the school community. While BIST was a program our district implemented in the late 90s, it had become watered-down and misused. We'd lost the pillars of grace and accountability. Through an extensive BIST reawakening, we became an "our kids" school. The systems of support for students, as well as one another, grew far beyond what we imagined to be possible. Restrictions with strong relationships, early intervention, and personalized skills-based coaching were foundational to our success. There was a true realization that teaching and protecting our students impacted them far beyond the walls of our classrooms. Marty Huitt and the BIST Model changed not only our school, but the lives of the people in it.

Mrs. Jennifer Kevern, Ed.S
Trailridge Elementary Principal
Lee's Summit, MO

This book is meant for any educator who has a heart for children who struggle. There have always been children in our school systems that struggle to meet expectations behaviorally. In the past, educators often looked for answers that might include different placements, special education identification, and mental health support. Over the course of time the number of children coming from chaos and often trauma has continued to increase. Then schools closed due to the pandemic in March of 2020. With the combination of the pandemic and the existing increased need of students, it became glaringly obvious that schools are so much more than "simply" institutions of academics. These two components magnified the need for schools to provide additional social emotional/behavioral support for high numbers of children.

This book is a guide for not only individual teachers, but also leadership teams. It will provide the needed philosophical foundation as well as the practical tools to help schools impact the whole child and no longer simply depend on outside resources for student success. (All charts and resources at the end of chapters can be applied in your own classroom and school). For schools to accomplish this, it is necessary that adults have strong, like-minded thinking about what children need to achieve at high levels. It also requires (in some cases) redefining success. Once the foundational "WHY" is in place for staff then the practical work begins.

Also provided are the "tools" to meet each child where they are and help them progress to the point that they are no longer dependent on the adults in the school for success. Likely some of the concepts and tools provided may already exist in your school community. However, it is the pervasiveness of like-minded thinking as well as the colleague support and collaboration that create success for children *and* adults. If you are passionate about change for children, change for educators, and change for school culture, this book is a must read!

"I Can't Help All of These Kids." Of Course You Can!

As a third-grade teacher with close to 20 years of experience at the elementary level, I can honestly say BIST will positively impact students' lives behaviorally and emotionally. Additionally, it can transform a teacher's way of thinking regarding student behavior if done purposefully, with fidelity, and a commitment to the BIST philosophy. When I first started teaching, my school utilized bits and pieces of BIST, but we didn't fully embrace it as a staff. That all changed several years later when a new principal was hired at my school, and he was a big advocate for BIST. He challenged our staff that if we say we do BIST, then we are going to commit to doing BIST philosophically as well as logistically.

I knew if I was going to successfully implement BIST in my classroom, then I needed my students to partner with me as we moved forward along this journey. In order to do that, I took time at the beginning of the year to share with my class what BIST is and why we are doing it. I taught my students the three goals for life and how they can help them in any area of their lives, not just at school. I taught them about gateway behaviors and the BIST continuum. I wanted my class to know I would help them with their behavior, and I would hold them accountable for their choices every time they made a mistake. It was important to me that my students understood the purpose of BIST is to help them not hurt them and to protect them not punish them. These are things I believe are incredibly important, and I make it a priority to teach them to my students each year.

"I Can't Help All of These Kids."

> Through my experiences I discovered I can't do BIST *to* students; I must do BIST *with* students if I truly want to change a child's behavior long term. This also helped me realize that there aren't bad kids but rather there are kids who make bad choices because of a missing skill they have in their life. My goal as a teacher is to protect, support, and help kids be successful in school not just academically but behaviorally and emotionally as well.
> I am a firm believer and a testament that the BIST Model works.
>
> Stephanie Mwansanga
> Trailridge Elementary, Third Grade Teacher
> Lee's Summit MO

"I think I might take a sick day tomorrow." "That kid keeps saying they're going to move. Is it ok if I hope that really happens?" "I didn't sleep at all last night – thinking about *that* student." "What can I do to help teachers with that hard kid?" If you have ever felt or heard these types of statements, keep reading.

"In the United States, 8 percent of teachers leave the profession annually, and more than 50 percent quit teaching before reaching retirement." (NASSP 2020).

One of the most common factors contributing to lack of teacher satisfaction is student behavior.

With a higher percentage of students coming from chaos and often trauma, behavior is a constant in numerous classrooms. If teachers are not given the skills to address behavior in a way that creates success, education will continue to see a high percentage of teachers looking elsewhere for a job that provides a sense of accomplishment.

In some of the schools that have implemented the Behavior Intervention Support Team (BIST) Model, there has been an increase not only in students' success, but in teacher satisfaction. This satisfaction comes through the common belief that all children are worthy of success and "we as a staff have the ability to help them experience this success." When the implementation process begins, the most notable attribute is increased calmness throughout the building as well as in individual classrooms. Additionally, teachers' ownership of students begins to increase as staff members see their obligation to each student in the building, not just the students in their classroom. Finally, students have an increased sense of pride due to their daily success in their ability to manage their "life skills."

History of BIST

The (BIST) Model is an outreach program of Ozanam within Cornerstones of Care. Ozanam is a residential and day treatment facility in the Kansas City, Missouri area. It was founded in 1948. Ozanam presently serves children and youth aged 5–23 both in the residential and in the therapeutic day treatment school. The BIST Model was developed by Nancy Osterhaus who was then serving as the administrator for Ozanam Day Treatment School. BIST was the model utilized to provide behavioral support for these students. It was extremely successful, and the students frequently achieved sustainable improvements. In 1990, to provide the much-needed support for vulnerable students in other schools, Osterhaus started training administrators and staff members in public, charter, and parochial schools to become more intentional and consistent in their support of struggling students. BIST, as an organization, continues to grow out of the need to help schools develop a systematic approach to effectively serve students who need support managing their behavior.

The goal is to help children develop new behavior strategies by educating them, their teachers, administrators, and parents. The BIST Model teaches students skills that allow them to make life-long positive changes. Adults actively and compassionately support the students as they learn and use their new skills. Providing adult support for these struggling students is key in creating and maintaining a healthy, learning environment.

BIST is a cognitive behavioral approach based on the balance of Grace and Accountability. (These concepts will be covered in depth later in this chapter.) By having a complete understanding of Grace and Accountability, adults can address and support the most challenging students in a direct, respectful manner. This comprehensive approach allows children to begin to trust the adults and develop coachable partnerships. When adults can remain calm and compassionate while working with children, they are able to guide students through the process of Accountability. By guiding students through this process educators can assist students in making significant, long-term, sustainable changes. Additionally, this process provides the opportunity for students to become better problem-solvers, increase their resilience, and overcome behavioral challenges. When educators can put these concepts into practice the opportunities for unlimited success exist.

"I Can't Help All of These Kids."

Working with difficult students can feel overwhelming and sometimes impossible. The information provided in the following chapters can also feel overwhelming. Schools that have been able to learn and then consistently implement this model have experienced high levels of success with difficult students. During the implementation process there will no doubt be bumps in the road. This is not a quick "fix" but rather a "marathon" meant to create sustainable change. It is often difficult and staff members at times may feel as if the work cannot practically be done. As a teacher, I had the opportunity to help lead the implementation of the BIST Model in the school in which I was teaching. During November of our first year, Nancy Osterhaus (the developer of the model) came to our building for problem solving support. When I saw her, she asked how things were going. My response was "Not good! I'm not even sure why we started this process." Fortunately, our building stayed the course and began to reap the benefits not only for children, but also for adults. Therefore, when there are struggles, come together with colleagues and talk through the concerns. Working together as a school community, this model can be implemented in a manner that increases success for children.

Why Are There So Many Behavior Problems?

Why do students get in trouble? Why do some kids never stop getting in trouble? Over the course of time there has been an increase in inappropriate behavior in classrooms. Statistics in the United States report that 7.8 million students are abused on an annual basis and every five hours a student is killed by abuse or neglect (americanspcc.org). These are staggering and shameful numbers. As Larry Brendtro and coauthors state in *Reclaiming Youth at Risk*: "Parents are too stressed, schools are too impersonal, and the community is too disorganized to fulfill the most basic human need of children to belong" (2002, p. 7).

Many students come to school and can follow directions and perform at a high level. However, a percentage of them are not able to meet classroom expectations and follow directions consistently. There are essentially three reasons why students get in trouble. The first reason is they don't know any better. If lack of information is the concern, teachers can provide clarity around information and good classroom management. The second reason students get in trouble is because they test limits. Educators know that consistency is critical in providing a strong learning environment. When students test limits, this can be addressed through relationships and structured, consistent classroom management. Third, students get in trouble because they can't manage their feelings. This is often due to one or more of the following:

- Abuse and neglect;
- Organic and neurological reasons;
- They are unattached or unbonded to significant adults;
- Complex trauma.

In addition to these significant concerns, some children can struggle due to a lack of consistent boundaries, overindulgence, or entitlement among other environmental circumstances.

When students can't manage feelings, teachers need to go beyond classroom management. For teachers to feel successful with these students, it will be important for the school to have a strong, philosophical foundation. Additionally, the ability of the staff to collaborate and problem solve student concerns in a manner that supports both the student and the teacher will be necessary.

Most adults can have an overwhelming feeling and then choose an appropriate behavior in response to that feeling. However, children who cannot manage emotions can have feelings and behaviors that are fused together. Some examples of this are:

- When a child is mad, they demonstrate behavior that gets them in trouble;
- When a child is bored, they become disruptive;
- When a child is embarrassed, they become defiant.

To ultimately impact change, adults must be able to help children separate their feelings from their negative behaviors.

Stress and trauma are affecting our students at alarming rates. As an example, 7.4% of children aged 3–17 have a diagnosed behavior problem (cdc.gov). Anxiety disorders affect 25.1% of students 13–18 years old (adaa.org). These experiences can change the way an individual's brain works. As stated in the book *Mindful School Communities* by Christine Mason and

"I Can't Help All of These Kids."

coauthors, there are challenges associated with childhood trauma and stress that compromise learning and teaching. By building compassionate, supportive school environments, educators learn to find balance between social-emotional health, well-being, and academic achievement. Schools that are aware of student trauma can increase empathy and support for students while maintaining expectations. The concept of providing support while maintaining expectations describes the BIST Model.

Pick Your Battles ... NOT

When identifying students with chronic behavior, often the frequency of the behavior is a greater indicator of concern than the severity of behavior. In other words, chronic behavior does not always mean the intensity of the behavior. Teachers must look at how frequently the behavior is occurring. A "chronic kid" is a student who doesn't just get in trouble; rather they *don't stop* getting in trouble. Often when behaviors are more covert and do not stop the learning of other students, teachers have been taught to ignore or "pick your battles." However, when a student does something that is not "OK" and the adult ignores the behavior, it is silent permission to continue that behavior. It is important that teachers learn to "pick their timing" of when to address the behavior as opposed to not addressing it at all.

Here are some guidelines to follow with students:

- If the behavior won't work on the job, it won't work in our school system.
- "Pick your timing" over "pick your battles."

A teacher's job is to be as demanding of students behaviorally as they are of them academically. Would a teacher allow a student to learn that 25 + 25 = 51? Would the teacher say "That is close enough"? When students make academic mistakes, teachers feel an obligation to address them. In fact, if a teacher did not address the minor academic mistakes, they would be viewed as failing the student. It becomes critical that teachers have the same mindset when addressing behavioral mistakes. When a school community can be demanding and set high behavioral standards, students are able to achieve at a higher level. When students achieve at a higher level, they have increased confidence and the result is frequently increased effort.

"I Can't Help All of These Kids."

Behaviors Must Be Taught

Think back to the reasons students can't manage feelings (abuse and neglect, organic and neurological reasons, being unattached or unbonded to significant adults, complex trauma, environmental circumstances). It is no wonder some students misbehave. When identifying chronic behaviors, the adult must go beneath the behavior and connect it to one or more missing skills. Which are:

1. I cannot experience an uncomfortable or overwhelming feeling without getting in trouble.
2. I cannot be OK if others are not OK.
3. I cannot do something when I don't want to, or it is hard.

If teachers can identify repetitive behaviors and connect them to a missing skill it can become a teachable attribute. By connecting student behavior to a life skill, two things can be accomplished:

1. Adults can be less emotional about misbehavior. When teachers perceive mistakes as behavior, it can frequently feel personal and as if the teacher has done something wrong. This can often cause the adults to feel emotional and sometimes defeated by that behavior. An example could be when a student gets mad and throws a book. If the teacher is focused solely on the poor behavior instead of the missing skill, frustration and inadequacy can come into play. However, if the adult can identify that this student does not know how to manage emotions in a productive manner, then there is a skill that can be taught.
2. Adults can be solution based and able to teach a new skill. By seeing behavioral mistakes as a missing skill as opposed to a choice, adults can narrow all behaviors down to three missing skills. This clarifies what must be taught. The focus can be on the solution of how to teach the individual student the skill they are missing.

This concept can shift the responsibility to a student's missing skill as opposed to a teacher's inadequacy. Teachers can reinstate hope for children by helping them recognize their struggle is about a missing skill as opposed to a character flaw. Additionally, this provides hope that change of behavior can be achieved through teaching skills. It is simply taking a teacher's expertise (teaching) and putting it into the area of behavior. It goes beyond modifying behavior to creating long-term change.

The missing skills are the foundation for the Three Goals for Life:

1. I can make good choices even if I am mad (or have an overwhelming feeling).
2. I can be okay even if others are not okay.
3. I can do something even if I don't want to (or if it's hard).

When schools can make the Goals for Life part of their foundational thinking about behavior it increases hope and energy in the adult community. This hope and energy can translate to more collaboration and expand the opportunity to create an "Our Kids" community. If teachers can view behavior as skill based, it can be taught. Academics are critical for student success. However, when thinking about children beyond school years, the Goals for Life are equally critical in success.

The Foundation of BIST

Grace

Every teacher entering education as a career knows that relationships will be a critical part of their success. In fact, this may be the draw for many teachers. For teachers to establish relationships that allow for coachability, it is important that each teacher understands the concept of Grace in the relationship. Teachers have the obligation to provide unconditional relationships with children. Grace is the provision of an unconditional relationship which means:

1. Providing what students need, not what they deserve.
2. Providing what students need when they want it and when they don't want it.

As more kids come from chaos or trauma, more look to teachers for their significant relationships. When helping teachers establish relationships that are significant and allow for student growth, it is important that all adults understand the steps of developing healthy relationships.

Anatomy of a Relationship

Relationships can have a huge impact on attitudes and the willingness to do what others ask. Many visualize the fun parts of relationships, the parts of connecting and associating with others. This is part of a relationship, but this is not the place to start with students. Boundaries are the starting point for strong, healthy relationships followed by connections and predictability. Relationships are the inception for change and growth.

- Boundaries: Consistent, firm boundaries are the number one element that must be in place. Boundaries must be initially communicated so the adult can define the guidelines or criteria for the environment. What is and is not OK to do and say? Here are two essential classroom boundaries:
  - It is never OK to be disruptive to learning. It is always OK to be a good learner and ask for help.
  - It is never OK to be hurtful. It is always OK to be a good friend and be kind.

  Boundaries are the beginning of trust. By establishing expectations and boundaries, the testing of limits can be reduced. Consistent, firm boundaries, delivered in a kind manner, can also increase security for many students who may live in a world of unpredictable or inconsistent boundaries.
- Connections: Genuine connections determine how people associate or attach with others. This is what makes a joyful classroom. The following traits help define a true connection:
  - Authenticity;
  - Sincerity;
  - Caring.

  In the article, Welcoming Students with a Smile by Youki Terada, she states that greeting kids at the classroom door using their name can increase engagement by 20% and decrease disruptive behavior by 9%, potentially adding an hour of academic engagement each day.
- Predictability: This increases the pace at which children can trust adults. It is established through consistent procedures and routines, as well as consistent adult responses to those expectations. Some questions for reflection are:
  - Are your boundaries consistent?
  - Are your emotions consistent when redirecting students?
  - Do you say what you mean and mean what you say?

Once boundaries, connections, and predictability are in place, teachers are well on their way to having effective relationships with their students. (Refer to the predictability activity at the end of the chapter.)

Student Rejection Cycle

They never talked about this in college!!! I graduated with my bachelor's degree mid-school year with a certification in Special Education (emphasis on behavior). I was determined to find a teaching position even though it was the second semester. I found one at Marillac Center for Children in Kansas City, MO. It was a residential, day treatment facility for emotionally disturbed children. I started my teaching career on January 2 of that school year, and I was ready to change the world one child at a time. Within six hours, I had been rejected in an overt way – a student spat on my face. My immediate response was: "They never talked about this in college!" And they didn't. So, I began my teaching career and within one school day felt deflated and wondered if I had chosen the correct occupation. How many teachers step into the classroom with that same energy of "I can change the world" and then quickly become disillusioned because they are not prepared for the personal rejection children can present? It is important that educators understand the reason behind those rejections and how to manage them in a manner that does not damage the relationship.

Sometimes the experiences students face can lead to the inability to trust adults. When a new positive role model or adult comes into their lives, the students' past experiences may cause them to automatically doubt this "trustworthy" adult. Many times, the student will emotionally hurt or be disrespectful to push the adults away. "Hurt people hurt people" (Will Bowen). This is one way by which students protect themselves from further adult rejection. In many situations, they would rather reject first before the adult can reject them.

When student rejection occurs, the typical response is "Don't take it personally." This is easier said than done. Adults must understand that by rejecting through misbehavior, students are testing to see if the adult will "stick" with them. Without this recognition, teachers will eventually pull away from the relationship out of self-preservation. When this happens, the adult loses the opportunity to coach that student through accountability.

Educators must learn to "lean in" and stay in the relationship even when students reject them. Staff words and actions need to say, "You can't be bad enough for me to give up on you." Educators must be courageous enough to address and stop the acting out behavior exhibited by the student (specific information on this is given later in this chapter). Relationship development, trust, and consistency are the underlying principles that allow teachers to be intrusive enough to stop students acting out. Once the acting out is stopped, work begins on shaping the new behavior. This can be done in a manner that does not erode the relationship.

Coaching

We identify a student's need by looking beyond the behavior to the life skill the student is missing. Behaviors can be tied to a skill that can be taught. Teachers cannot successfully coach or teach from a distance; staff must coach students when they are physically and emotionally "close." Trustworthy adults must lean in and stay in the relationship until the student can accept help.

The famous football coach, Tom Landry, defines coaching as:

- Someone who tells you what you don't want to hear;
- Asks you to do things you don't want to do;
- So you can be who you have always known you can be.

For educators, the last statement has been adjusted to "so you can become the person you are worthy of being."

Accountability

Accountability is the foundation of change and is defined as the ability to reflect, be honest, and problem solve for improvement. Relationships alone do not create significant change. They provide the opportunity for students to be vulnerable with adults. Vulnerability is required for individuals to be reflective. This reflection in conjunction with coaching and support can allow students to move through the five levels of accountability (see below), therefore allowing for long term change.

The word Accountability often creates the image of punishment. This could not be further from the truth as it is the foundation for any long-term, significant change. True Accountability is the kindest gift we can provide to students. However, because it is so hard to experience, it must be facilitated through kindness. Staff must truly understand the meaning of and have the ability to guide the process of Accountability.

"I Can't Help All of These Kids."

When working with students who repeatedly struggle with behavior, punishment will not create long-term change and will ultimately increase student resistance. To create this long-term change teachers must be able to provide an environment where students feel safe while problem solving new solutions.

There are five levels to accountability, as follows.

1. **I did it**. This is the level of honesty and admission. If a student cannot admit that they have created a problem, they will not be able to change as the problem was not theirs.
2. **I'm sorry**. This is the level in which adults are asking students to identify the problem they created through their actions. Teachers might initially identify this level as one that would include an apology, but it is, rather, an identification of how their actions impacted others.
3. **It's a problem in my life**. This level of accountability is the foundation of change. The adults must be able to help students see that their actions are bigger than a one-time incident. The adults also help students to identify the pattern of their behavior that is inhibiting their success. Additionally, it will be critical for the adult to connect the behaviors to a life skill in order to have impact beyond the classroom.
4. **I accept consequences**. This level requires the student to accept restrictions to protect them from getting in trouble. This is not related to a handbook consequence, but rather related to the student's inability.
5. **I accept and need help**. This is the level that allows true change to begin. At this level, an adult will coach a student on a new life skill and create opportunities for practice to ensure acquisition and mastery of the new skill. This mastery must be at a level that will allow students to eventually experience success without the restrictions or protections that were originally implemented.

What is required: Guiding students through accountability is time consuming and takes intentional thought and skill. When adults can consistently guide students through this process it can be one of the most rewarding actions teachers experience when working with difficult students. Accountability is the kindest gift adults can provide to children. By embarking on this vulnerable journey, adults have the opportunity to not only create increased success in the classroom, but also in life. The journey of Accountability requires three components from the adults.

1. **Time**: It is important to understand that Accountability and problem-solving conversations can only be done when both individuals are calm and can be logical thinkers. This requires the gift of time to be given to students (and sometimes adults). In the daily hustle of teaching, this can feel monumental and frustrating. However, if the process is rushed and either individual is still emotional, the conversation will not be effective and can delay the experience of Accountability.

    The two ways to avoid Accountability are denial and blame. When adults are aware of this, they can assess the readiness for this conversation through the student's ability to be honest about their actions. More time may be needed if a student continues to blame others or denies that their actions were of concern. When providing additional time, restrictions may be needed to protect the student from further negative behavior.

2. **Relationship**: Adults frequently struggle with true Accountability in their own lives. It is a struggle for individuals to look at themselves and admit the flaws in their behavior. If adults can recognize this difficulty, it allows for increased empathy and understanding when guiding students through this process. Because Accountability is so hard, it is critical that the student being supported can trust the relationship they have with the adult. Students must be able to trust that when the adult sees the negative impact of their behavior the adult will not abandon them. The adult must be able to assure the student that what they are dealing with is part of being human and that with adult support change can be achieved. True Accountability requires vulnerability. When adults are able to model this, it can increase the student's willingness to also be vulnerable enough to proceed through the journey of Accountability.

3. **Questions**: When students have created a problem, the traditional response from adults is to restate the unmet expectations in the form of a lecture. There is minimal buy-in when listening to a lecture even if the information delivered is valid and kind. Accountability is a problem-solving conversation that is question-based in order to increase student ownership. The Accountability for students comes through the ability to answer questions, own the problem they created, and recognize the concerns.

When guiding students in this conversation, it is ideal if it occurs in private and one on one. The conversation cannot be made in anger as this will increase student resistance.

The process should be comparable to a problem-solving conversation that a teacher would have with a student who is struggling academically. It is calm, kind, and intentional, thus allowing students to leave the conversation with hope and a plan to implement more successful actions.

Accountability is a journey not a one-time conversation. Adults must understand that children are changing habits that may have been in place for numerous years. It requires that teaching and protecting continue beyond the problem-solving conversation. Adults should look for three big rocks to measure a student's progress: ownership, partnership, and coachability:

- **Ownership**: This is the student's ability to own the problem they created. This requires going beyond simple honesty to being able to recognize the impact of the behavior and accept that their actions created a problem.
- **Partnership**: This is the student's ability to work with the adult and put forth the same level of effort toward change that the adult is providing.
- **Coachability**: This is a student's willingness to receive feedback and direction in specific situations without making it worse.

A student must be able to own the problem and partner with the adult in a way that allows the adult to coach them in a new skill. Knowing that accountability is a journey, adults must understand that students will continue to make mistakes. Thus, a student's progress is not determined by a lack of mistakes, but rather by their effort to do things differently. This entire process requires stamina and resilience not only on the part of the student, but more importantly on the part of the adult.

Table 1.1 helps to visualize the connection between the Three Big Rocks and the Five Levels of Accountability.

Table 1.1 Three Big Rocks of Accountability and Five Levels of Accountability

Big Rocks of Accountability	Five Levels of Accountability
Ownership	I did it
Partnership	I'm sorry
	It's a problem in my life
Coachability	I accept consequences
	I accept and need help

Teach and Protect

Since one of the most emotional topics in schools is student behavior, these behaviors can leave teachers feeling inadequate and frustrated, and thus create a sense of defeat and eventually rejection of the student. When schools have students that are constantly misbehaving, the actions taken by staff are typically punishment based. Unfortunately, the result of punishment-based actions rarely results in long-term change. When the behavior recurs, the adult response increases in length. (Example: 45-minute detention to Saturday school.) This process starts the cycle of student resistance and teacher frustration. If schools want to increase teacher confidence and success when working with students who struggle, they must embrace the concepts of teaching and protecting.

Teaching is about changing a child's skillset to increase their success. Typically, this thinking is focused on academic content. However, what if educators took that same statement and changed the focus to behavior? When a student does not know how to read, we teach them. When a student does not know how to be angry without getting in trouble, teaching a new coping skill is the long-term solution.

Protecting is about changing the environment to stop misbehavior. An academic example of this is modification of an assignment. A behavioral example is when a student cannot play successfully on the playground. We then assign an area where they are allowed to play safely during recess.

Our ultimate goal with students who struggle is to balance teaching (changing a skillset = internal) with protecting (restricting what a student can't manage = external) to allow for long-term change. To accomplish this goal, adults must be able to first stop acting out behavior through protections/restrictions and then teach a new skill so that a student can manage any environment.

Protection vs. Punishment

When a student struggles with behavior the school's traditional response is to give the student a consequence. The consequence is meant to provide some level of displeasure and therefore the student will not repeat the action. This is the definition of punishment. Punishment can be a valid response to student actions. However, when the student is repetitious in their behavior, punishments grow in time and severity, and this typically

"I Can't Help All of These Kids."

Table 1.2 Punishment and Protection

Punishment	Protection
Time based	Skill based
Based on school handbook	Based on what a student can't manage
We do it to you	We do it for you and with you
Designated end time	Increased skills determine timeframe
Fresh start after end of punishment	Ongoing coaching and support

results in the student becoming more adversarial with the adults. It also results in increased adult frustrations with that specific student. The vicious cycle of punishment and forgiveness has started. Once this cycle has started, two things tend to happen: (1) by February the teacher(s) have given up on that student and (2) the student loses hope that they can change.

Protection is changing a student's environment in order to stop them from acting out. It is limiting or removing access to what the student can't manage, or to keep them safe. Once the acting out stops, adults must then teach and coach students around the new skills.

- **First example of punishment**: A student continues to talk to friends in class, so the teacher makes her walk laps for ten minutes on the playground during recess. Once the ten minutes are complete, the punishment is over, and the student can return to recess.
- **First example of protection**: A student continues to talk to friends in class so the teacher changes seating to limit the opportunity for talking.
- **Second example of punishment**: A secondary student is impulsive and out of bounds during passing periods and comes to class very unfocused. The adults assign a detention for this hallway behavior.
- **Second example of protection**: A secondary student is impulsive and out of bounds during passing periods and comes to class very unfocused. The student is restricted from passing periods by implementing delayed passing.

Teaching vs. Strategies

When a student is identified as needing additional behavior support, frequently schools immediately put strategies in place based on a pre-existing menu of supports. There are two flaws with this thinking: (1) the support may not match the true need of the student; (2) there is a lack of teaching new skills.

First example of traditional strategies: When a student does not have academic stamina, the adult puts a break in place. The break is often outside the classroom and may create secondary gains.

First example of teaching a new skill: When the student needs to gain academic stamina, the adult helps them with the words to ask for assistance. (Example: "I need help when you are available." "I need a break for a minute.") Additionally, if a break is included, there is teaching around what it looks like to continue to work and how to push yourself to stay focused. As stamina grows the length of the break is reduced. Frequent practice of how to ask for assistance as well as continued work on stamina to stay focused are part of teaching a new skill.

Second example of traditional strategies: When a student cannot manage anger, they are often given a pass to exit the room. When the student does not use the pass correctly, or manipulates to leave the room, teachers become frustrated.

Second example of teaching a new skill: When a student cannot be angry without getting in trouble, they are taught how to use their words and actions to remain productive. (Example: "I feel angry, can I move to the safe seat?") This teaching must include timing of when to use their words, exact words to use, the tone of voice to use, and where to go to calm down. By teaching how to articulate with words and what appropriate actions should be, the opportunity to manipulate is minimized. Additionally, this will require frequent practice of the words and actions when the student is non-emotional.

The strategy of using an anger pass can be beneficial. However, it is also critical that students are taught how to use their words to let adults know how they feel as opposed to using manipulation to get their needs met. Strategies must be combined with teaching.

In summation, teaching and protecting are both critical components to long-term change. However, protection (environmental change) must be implemented prior to teaching (internal change). The student will not be able to learn a new skill if the acting out behavior continues. The environmental change will *stop* the behavior, the teaching of the new skill will

"I Can't Help All of These Kids."

Table 1.3 Strategies and Teaching

Strategies	Teaching
Based on menu of supports	Based on individual student needs
Strategy only	Teaching when and how to use the strategy
Immediate response to need	Long-term change based on life skill
Might not match true needs	Based on student's missing skill
Teacher led	Student owned

change the behavior. Schools are passionate about supporting students; however, the support is often incomplete. The adult community must ultimately be driven by the mindset of teaching *and* protecting.

Discipline in the Balance

If one has ever driven on a freshly graveled country road, it is well known how treacherous it can be. If sucked into one ditch by the loose gravel often the driver will overcompensate and end up in the opposite ditch. When working with difficult students this is the analogy that frequently occurs. Just like on a country road the goal is to stay between the ditches. One ditch can be labeled as enabling, the opposite ditch is labeled as counter-aggressive. The goal when working with students who struggle is to avoid both ditches.

When working with children that exhibit behavior concerns human nature can frequently lead to adults utilizing some of the responses listed in Table 1.4. If adults are not able to stay balanced in their approach with students, one of two things will happen: (1) if there is too much enabling behavior the adult will feel exhausted and frustrated because they are working harder than the student; (2) if there is too much counter-aggressive behavior

Table 1.4 Enabling and Counter-aggression

Enabling	Counter-aggression
Lecturing	Blaming others
Explaining	Predicting failure
Giving reasons why	Getting emotional
Rescuing	Choosing punishment
Ignoring behavior	Abandoning the relationship

in the interactions, the student will become adversarial and not trust that the adult is on their side.

If the adult is enabling initially, this often leads to the next interaction being counter-aggressive. In reverse, if the initial response is counter-aggressive, the second response is often enabling.

This diminishes predictability for the student. Adults can frequently find themselves on an "emotional roller coaster" with these students and become exhausted, lose hope of change, and eventually abandon the relationship under the guise of "I have tried everything I know." At this point, the adult has lost their ability to coach that student and the student is then stuck in their misbehavior and feels rejected by the adult.

To avoid this all-too-frequent scenario, adults must have an understanding that chronic misbehavior is driven by a missing life skill and the skill must be taught in order to create improvement. There are a few key components that adults must put in place to stay balanced while supporting difficult students:

- **Early intervention**: Adults must set specific expectations for each activity and address and stop out-of-bounds behavior quickly with only one individual, verbal redirect.
- **Protections**: Adults must identify what a student can't manage and put appropriate restrictions or protections in place to stop the acting out.
- **Accountability**: Adults must be willing to get beyond student denial and blame to guide the problem-solving process. This will begin the journey of Accountability.
- **Missing skill**: Adults must identify, teach, and practice the behavioral skill the student is missing.

End of Chapter Reflection and Questions

- **How does the definition of Accountability vary from what you presently do in your building? (How do you currently hold students accountable in your building?)**
- **How would you articulate the difference between protection and punishment?**

- **How would you articulate the difference between strategies and teaching new skills?**
- **Predictability activity**:

    One idea to assess predictability in the classroom is to have teachers or grade level teams do a consistency chart. At a minimum, teachers should strive to complete a consistency chart once a quarter. The basics of a consistency chart are simple: at the top of the chart in the first row place the schedule or agenda, class periods, activities, times, etc. Below in the left column place a list of all the students' names. Every time a student is redirected, a tally will be recorded under their name in that time period. Teachers should have a collaborative, follow up conversation regarding these questions:
    - Who are the students that were redirected too frequently?
    - What portion of the hour or day needs to be tightened?
    - What is the gender of the students being redirected?
    - What is the race of the students being redirected?
    - What is the socio-economic status?
    - Are there equity concerns?
    - What is my takeaway?

References

Bowen, Will, 2009. *Complaint free relationships: Transforming your life one relationship at a time*. New York City, NY: Doubleday Religion.

Brendtro, Larry K., Brokenleg, Martin and Van Bockern, Steve, 2002. *Reclaiming youth at risk: Our hope for the future*. Bloomington, IN: Solution Tree.

Landry, Tom, 1991. *Tom Landry: An autobiography*. New York City, NY: Harper.

Mason, Christine, Rivers Murphy, Michele M. and Jackson, Yvette, 2020. *Mindful school communities: The 5 C's of nurturing heart centered learning*. Bloomington, IN: Solution Tree.

NASSP.org, Jan 2020. *How school leadership effects teacher retention*. Vol 20. Principal Leadership. Boiling Springs, NC.

Terada, Youki, September, 2018. *Welcoming students with a smile*. Nicasio, CA: Edutopia.

Now What?

I have worked in education for 20+ years and every one of those years has been in special education with an emphasis in social development and behavioral support. I have passionately implemented the BIST Model not as an instructional strategy to improve classroom management, but as a decision-making philosophy that changes kids (and people's) lives.

So many years of our educational history has been dedicated to helping the classroom "decrease" the amount of interference that might get in the way of instruction. Some of the questions that continue to nag teachers are:

- Can we help a student showing troubling behaviors move from being attentive 15 minutes of class time to 20 minutes?
- Can we tangibly, positively reinforce with a "food item" what we want to see enough to create habits that will last?
- How can we help form a compliant classroom that will allow for instruction to take place without interruption?

I am grateful that the BIST philosophy takes a different approach and supports decision-making in general. BIST does not attempt to decrease the negative behaviors seen in a classroom (although side note, behaviors do decrease). The BIST philosophy strives to empower kids to make decisions right for them so that they can be successful within a classroom setting, community, employment agency and all other facets of life. The BIST philosophy is less concerned about the "what, how, when, and where" logistics of the behavior and trying to environmentally control the problem. It is more concerned about the "why" and supporting a student with making the best behavioral decision for them because it will improve their quality of life.

Now What?

> A portion of our building supports day-treatment students. Our students come to us with the hope that they can eventually return to the more generalized environment once they learn strategies for decision making and demonstrate ongoing safety. We have transitioned over 50 students back to home schools over the last 7 years, utilizing the BIST philosophy to guide our effort. When students' transition, our partner schools always ask, "What tangible reinforcers do we need to use to keep this success going?"; or "Tell us about the detailed behavior intervention plan that a teacher will need to follow to ensure the student continues to succeed in the classroom." We continually tell our partner schools that "our kids do not need the Skittles [candy] to improve their decision making." Thanks to BIST our kids know their "why" in making the right decision.
>
> Mr. Kelly Twenter
> Miller Park (Alternative Education/Day Treatment) Principal
> Lee's Summit, MO

Now that the foundation for adult thinking has been established, this chapter will focus on creating a pyramid of success to meet the needs of *all* children more effectively. This section will start with common area expectations which are needed to create a calmness in the building. Additionally, there will be a focus on classroom management to create predictability. And last, how to support individual students with missing skills so they can experience success. As schools address and implement these logistical concepts it is critical that all actions are driven by thinking based on Grace and Accountability, the foundation of the BIST Model. Adults become

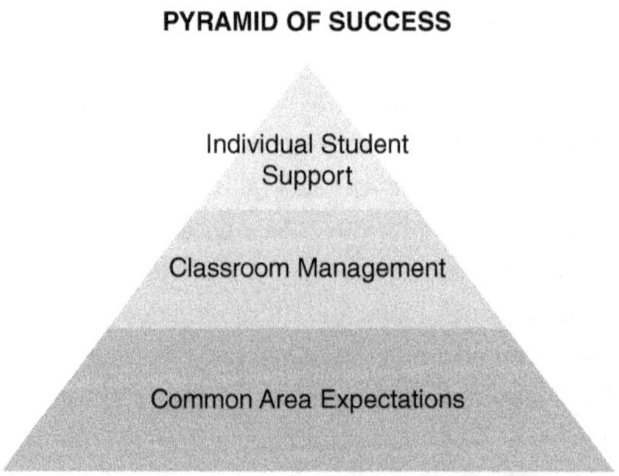

PYRAMID OF SUCCESS

- Individual Student Support
- Classroom Management
- Common Area Expectations

Figure 2.1 Pyramid of Success

predictable when guided by the belief that all children need a significant relationship while receiving guidance to problem solve mistakes.

The pyramid of success portrays how student behavioral supports are tiered in a building.

Clarity on Common Area Expectations

Most buildings understand the need for common area expectations (CAE) and spend a significant amount of time at the beginning of each school year on this work. Schools typically do a great job of enforcing CAE with energy and consistency initially. However, that energy of enforcement tends to drastically diminish by mid-fall. This is when adults get tired, feel that students should know and follow expectations, and therefore can become less engaged in supervision. These areas are frequently omitted but are needed to increase sustainability:

- How adults will respond when students are out of procedure;
- Conciseness around adult expectations;
- How adults will support and address each other when their expectations are not met.

Here are the four questions to consider when developing expectations for both students and adults. Bulleted with each question are points of consideration when answering the questions.

- What are the specific student expectations?
    - Specificity allows adults to stop students at a procedural level as opposed to a behavioral situation. This allows quicker compliance and increases consistency. Example: Students who carry a two-strap backpack are expected to have both arms through the straps. If one arm comes out and an adult intervenes it is procedural. If the adult does not stop the student until the backpack is swinging in the air and perhaps hits another student, that is behavioral.
    - Points of consideration:
        - Clarity of expectations allows students to stay in procedure;
        - Specificity decreases anxiety for students.

- How do adults intervene when students don't meet the expectations?
    - Predictable adult responses increase the pace at which students can trust not only their teacher(s) but the entire adult community.
    - Points of consideration:
        - Interventions must be driven by the same intentions from all adults;
        - Common interventions create quicker compliance and increase calmness;
        - Supervision is the most significant prevention.
- What are the specific adult expectations?
    - Adults must know exactly what is expected while supervising to be intentional and vigilant.
    - Points of consideration:
        - Adults need to greet and assess students emotionally as they enter the building;
        - Adult presence should say: We care about you, we want you here, and the adults here will be kind and in charge.
- How do we respond when the adults don't meet expectations?
    - Adults typically have the right intentions, but actions don't always match. In order to ensure actions stay at a high level, teacher teams must be able to lift each other up and help colleagues remain engaged and intentional.
    - Points of consideration:
        - Colleagues address and support each other;
        - Principals and directors confront, coach, and evaluate.

(Refer to Appendix 2.1.)

Classroom Management

The strategies presented by BIST should not be viewed as a replacement for classroom management, as they are not the same. Classroom management consists of procedures and routines developed by an individual teacher in their classroom. These procedures and routines are implemented to provide predictability for every student. The philosophy of BIST (Grace and

Accountability) should be present for every student in every interaction. However, the logistics of this model (safe seat/buddy room, planning) are needed when an individual student's behavior goes beyond a teacher's procedures and routines.

In this section, some of the components of effective classroom management are detailed. This is not a book about classroom management, but rather a section on how strong procedures and routines allow teachers to meet the needs of the majority of students. The BIST Model is a philosophy that has logistical components. Therefore, Grace and Accountability will be a part of every interaction. However, the logistics do not take the place of good classroom management.

If there is no clarity between BIST logistics and classroom management, teachers run the risk of using BIST as their management. If this occurs they may feel like every student is out of bounds. By using strong management teachers can identify the few students who are missing skills and need additional support.

It must be noted that with an increasing number of students who have experienced chaos and trauma, teachers must become even more intentional about establishing structures that provide boundaries, procedures, and routines within their classrooms. This predictability and consistency allow the majority of students to get their needs met. The following are the key components in establishing strong classroom management.

1. Preparation: *Fail to plan, plan to fail.*
    a. Room is ready – arranged in a manner that allows teachers to supervise all areas and includes visual cues for procedures and routines.
    b. Teacher is ready – has a daily plan of what must be accomplished.
    c. Work is ready – books, papers, assignments, and materials are accessible.
    d. Mindset is ready – have a positive attitude and enjoy the students.
2. Organization: *A place for everything, everything in its place.*
    a. Label things in the room for easy recognition and access.
    b. Color code folders and baskets for classroom organization.

Now What?

   c. Prepare a system for turning in daily assignments and picking up assignments when absent.
   d. Provide visual cues for class daily schedule and assignments for day/week.
3. Expectations: *Expectations are determined by what helps students achieve, not by what they have experienced.*
   a. It is always OK to be a good learner and ask for help.
   b. It is always OK to be a good friend and be kind.
4. Procedures/routines: *Procedures are your roadmap to meet your expectations.*
   a. Write out procedures in advance.
   b. Teach students the procedures.
   c. Show students how the procedures should and should not be performed.
   d. Have students practice the procedure until they master it.
   e. Monitor students' progress and re-teach over time.
5. Presence: *Teacher presence in a classroom can give students a sense of calm and safety.* Our presence needs to say three things to our students.
   a. "I've got this, you don't need to worry." Body language and words communicate to students that the teacher is in charge.
   b. "Say what you mean and mean what you say." Students must trust that you will follow through on what you have stated.
   c. "You as a student can't be bad enough to get rid of me." Tell your students both through words and actions that you will not give up on them and mean it.

(Refer to Appendices 2.2 and 2.3.)

Gateway Behaviors

One way to establish high expectations is through teaching and addressing gateway behaviors to all students. Gateway behaviors are often negative, non-verbal communication by students that let the adults know that they may not be OK. There are many different gateway behaviors.

Some of them include tapping pencils, eye rolling, moving slowly when directed to hurry, and body language. There are numerous other behaviors that can be added to this list. Gateway behaviors are mostly covert (not outrageous) but need to be addressed in order to set the expectations and diminish contagious behavior. Presenting and addressing gateway behaviors allows adults to confront behavior that could become something hurtful or disruptive.

What is the difference between being nit-picky and having high expectations? Being nit-picky can make students feel defeated based on a teacher's style of intervention and tone of voice.

Having high expectations helps students understand acceptable behaviors and know what must be done to achieve success. The difference is all about the intention in which the behaviors are redirected.

If teachers allow non-verbal, negative communication in the classroom three things are likely to happen:

1. Teachers will become frustrated with students;
2. Individual students will become more resistive to adult directions;
3. The behavior can become contagious in the classroom.

Teaching students about gateway behaviors increases student awareness about non-verbal communication and the impression that can be communicated without words. Our ultimate goal is to help students use their words not their actions to get their needs met.

When teaching about gateway behaviors, here are five considerations with examples:

1. Define gateway behaviors as part of a class meeting. Allow students to participate in developing a list of these behaviors.
    - "I have noticed some behaviors that might be considered negative or disrespectful. I want us to talk about non-verbal communication and how people might perceive you when you're not using your words. Here are some examples of things I have seen: eye rolling when students don't like what is said, moving slowly when directed to do something quickly, etc. At your table in a shoulder voice volume, please discuss other possible behaviors that tell people you don't like what has been stated. You have five minutes for discussion."
2. Increase class understanding about why these behaviors will be addressed.
    - "Who in this class can tell me why I am going to make a big deal out of the behaviors we have identified?" Ideally, students will be able to state why teachers are addressing these small, non-verbal actions. By

asking the students to identify the why, it increases their buy in and ownership. The student response should include "We do not allow unkind or disrespectful behavior to occur in the classroom."
3. Teach students how the adult will address individuals when a gateway behavior occurs (either at the time or later). Below is an example of language that can be utilized in these situations.
    - "Are you OK, I don't want you to be in trouble."
4. Teach students how to respond when addressed by an adult regarding a gateway behavior.
    - "The appropriate response is a respectful 'yes' and then get back on track."
5. Teach students what is expected if they are not able to respond correctly.
    - "If you are not able to respond appropriately, I might ask you to go to the safe seat. You are not in trouble; I just want you to be aware of what you are saying without your words."

Consistency

Systems vs. Individual

All schools know that consistency is a critical ingredient for success. In fact, frequently when working with schools I hear staff members state: "We need more consistency." What does this mean and is it achievable? In order to create a truly consistent environment, it is important to recognize that consistency must be developed in two areas: system consistency and individual student consistency.

System consistency includes school common area expectations, classroom management, and common language that is used throughout the building. These supports are predictable and help to provide calmness in the school. Student and teacher expectations must be clear and concise. To remain committed to the enforcement of system consistency, team leaders must reinforce staff's beliefs regarding the criticalness of calmness.

Once schools have implemented consistent systems, there will still be students who have additional needs. It is the school's obligation to consider how to support students on an individual basis. This is the second component of consistency in a building: *individual consistency*. To develop a high level of individual consistency schools must look at every child's needs to help them achieve success. Individual consistency is defined by two different levels:

- Redirecting behavior in classrooms;
- Identifying support for individual students.

Redirecting Behavior in Classrooms

When teachers address behavior in the classroom, they can often feel "stuck" with what to do with the student. The behavior may not be at the level of an office referral, but it certainly must be addressed and stopped. A *thinking flow chart* can help teachers have confidence and remain logical and solution based when addressing behaviors.

Thinking Flow Chart

1. *What action should I take to stop this behavior?* The "why" behind this question is that it allows the teacher to stop the behavior in a manner that is best for that student and the classroom in that situation, which may not be the safe seat (defined in Chapter 3). At the moment of intervention, the goal is to stop the behavior with the least amount of resistance from the student and the least amount of disruption to the classroom.
2. *What does the student need academically at the moment when stopping the behavior?* The "why" for this question is for the teacher to think about how to get the student back on track. When the behavior has stopped, the adult needs to look at replacing the unwanted behavior with an academic activity. This does not mean that the teacher's sole focus is on this student; however, the goal is to help the redirected student continue to be a part of the learning environment. As examples, a teacher might point to the section in the book in which they are working or provide an activity for the student to work on if they have moved to a new location.
3. *What skill is the student missing?* The "why" for this question allows the teacher to be solution based as opposed to problem based. By connecting the behavior to a skill, the adult is more likely to remain logical instead of emotional about the student's behavior.

4. *When can I follow up with the student to problem solve/process?* The "why" for this last question helps the teacher to mentally plan a time to follow up with the student to problem solve. By having a plan in mind, the teacher can continue teaching the remainder of the class.

When teachers can think through the four questions listed above, it allows them to consistently meet the needs of students when redirecting behavior. Even though actions are different, intentions remain consistent.

Identifying Support for Individual Students

Consistency in this area comes from looking at each student as an individual and doing what is needed for that student instead of doing the same thing for each of them. An example of this is when a school puts every child who struggles on a "check in and check out" routine. This is frequently used as the first "step" for struggling students. However, not every student needs or benefits from this type of support. An effective method for consistency with individual students is to answer these four questions:

1. What does the student's repetitious behavior tell us they can't manage?
2. What restrictions does the student need to stop the behavior based on what they can't manage?
3. What skill do we need to teach and practice?
4. How and when do we reduce restrictions?

If teachers are able to consider these four questions, they are then able to consistently meet the needs of individual students who need support beyond classroom management.

Providing What Students Need

There are four steps or actions for adults to take to provide students with what they need to be successful in school. In order for these four steps to be effective, Grace and Accountability must be in place:

1. Early intervention: **WHEN** to intervene;
2. Caring confrontation: **HOW** to intervene;

3. Protective planning: **WHAT** to do to support students when early intervention and caring confrontation are not enough;
4. Outlasting the acting out: the journey of holding students accountable to create a life change.

Early Intervention

"Stop the behavior **when** you see it, don't wait until you feel it." To be effective with early intervention a teacher must be willing to address behavior individually and verbally only one time per activity and then take action to stop it. The goal of early intervention is to stop the behavior so that teaching and learning can continue. By using early intervention, the adult can address students without emotion. This can increase the opportunity for quick compliance allowing learning to continue. If adults use emotion, the chance of students mirroring that emotion increases. This will hinder the student's ability to look at their own behavior. Additionally, early intervention utilized throughout the building will increase predictability among adults. This can decrease the need for students to test the boundaries of different adults.

The two main guidelines to follow when intervening are:

- It is never OK to be disruptive – it is always OK to be a good learner and ask for help.
- It is never OK to be hurtful – it is always OK to be kind and be a good friend.

Teachers will continue to use non-verbal techniques such as proximity, putting a hand on the student's desk, getting eye contact with the student, or using the quiet signal. If the non-verbal redirect does not work, the teacher will use an individual, verbal redirect. If that does not stop the behavior, the adult will take additional action that ensures the behavior stops and the class learning continues. (Refer to the thinking flow chart above.)

Caring Confrontation

Confronting student behavior can evoke emotion simply due to not being able to predict a student's response. When school communities are in the process of establishing their philosophical foundation, creating common language when addressing students can be a significant tool for growth and cohesiveness. There are many benefits of developing a common language: (1) it reduces adult emotion during a confrontation; (2) it allows adults to address students in a predictable manner; (3) it gains student compliance more quickly; and (4) it increases student trust of multiple adults.

How the behavior is stopped can make all the difference in the student response. The goal is to create common language around interventions throughout the entire staff. Common language does not mean that a teacher's individual style is diminished. Teacher personality is critical in the development of relationships and plays an important role when redirecting student behavior. When confronting a student verbally, the words used should be delivered in this manner:

- Quick;
- Kind;
- Calm;
- Firm;
- Close.

The teacher's intention when redirecting behavior is for their presence to say: "I will always be on your side. I will never let you be out of bounds because you are worthy of success."

One way to redirect is to use the ICE statement:

- "I see … [disruptive behavior]"
- "Can you … [desired behavior]"
- "Even though … [student's feeling]"

For example: "I see you are having trouble standing in line. Can you keep your hands to yourself even though it might be hard?" This specific language is important for students who tend to escalate quickly and for students who need control. Although the teacher may intervene in an appropriate manner, it does not ensure student compliance. The appropriate delivery of the redirect simply ensures that the teacher is not part of the problem.

Student responses to adult redirection are predictable when students are resistant: see Table 2.1.

Table 2.1 Student Reactions and Adult Responses

Student Reactions	Adult Responses
Shut down	Set limits and follow through
Denial: "Why? What did I do?"	"Great question. Can you go ahead and …?"
Blaming: "He did it too, I'm not the only one."	"This is really hard. Can you go ahead and …?"

For adults to be ready with a predictable response, it is helpful to remember possible student reactions. This pre-planning allows adults to follow through without emotion. This skill takes practice on the part of the adults.

Protective Planning

Writing a plan for success is *what* teachers do to support children with repetitious, out-of-bounds behaviors when early intervention and caring confrontation are not enough. These plans create predictability and consistency for students and staff allowing students to know what will happen with their disruptive or hurtful behaviors.

The development of an individual plan should occur after a student has experienced three behavior incidents in a month or less. By providing support after only three concerns allows the adult community to intervene early, put support in place, and teach a new skill to increase success.

When a student goes beyond classroom management, support should be a tiered system (Mattos et al., 2009):

1. Teacher provides support in the classroom.
2. Teacher meets with the grade level or team to brainstorm additional strategies.
3. Teacher involves a member of the Vision Team to help support problem-solving regarding that student.
4. Teacher contacts the RTI/CARE/MTSS/SAT team that would identify if there is a need for special education consideration or an FBA (Functional Behavioral Analysis).

Students, parents, and school personnel are all involved in creating the plan for success. At a minimum, parents *must* be aware of the plan. If parent communication is omitted, it increases the opportunity for polarization between school and home. The goal is to have parents and staff working together towards student success. Plans should be reviewed on a three to four week basis and modified when the student is not progressing.

When developing a plan, the teachers involved should answer the following questions prior to meeting with the student (as previously listed in identifying support for individual students):

1. What does the student's repetitious behavior tell us they can't manage?
2. What restrictions does the student need to stop the behavior based on what they can't manage?
3. What skill do we need to teach and practice?
4. How and when do we reduce restrictions?

   (For additional questions to utilize when developing a plan, refer to Appendix 2.4.)

This allows the team to start with the end in mind. Instead of presenting the student with a completed plan, the development should occur in partnership with the student. This helps with ownership and buy-in.

During the meeting, one teacher does the talking and sits beside the student. The meeting starts by saying: "You're not in trouble, we want to do a better job of helping you." The meeting is question based. (Refer to Appendix 2.5.)

The other teachers are observers and talk minimally throughout the planning meeting. They can take notes, keep time, and record thoughts to discuss after the meeting is completed.

However, it is important for the student to see all adults involved as being on their side. Multiple adults being in attendance demonstrates support of the student and decreases opportunity to manipulate.

There are specific components that should be considered in the student's plan. (Refer to Appendix 2.7 and 2.8) They are:

1. Identify the skill to teach
   a. Some students are missing all three goals for life (refer to Chapter 1). When planning for a student, pick one goal to focus on initially.

2. Plan when and how to teach and practice the missing skill (teaching)
   a. Students will need to be taught this skill. Practice will also need to occur on a frequent basis for the student to gain mastery of this skill. (Refer to Appendix 2.6.)
3. Specific restrictions to protect the student (protecting)
   a. This requires looking at what the student can't manage and putting restrictions in place to protect them.
   b. When restrictions are put in place relationships must be increased. If relationships are not concurrently increased with restrictions, students will become adversarial toward adults and resist change.
4. Progress monitoring through targeted behaviors
   a. Targeted behaviors are identified and tracked to monitor if there is a decrease in the unwanted behavior
5. Contribution in the school community
   a. The purpose of student contribution is to increase their confidence, belonging, empathy, significance, or skill competence.
   b. Contribution is a critical component for numerous students. When implementing contribution, it can be tempting to only allow a student to participate if they are meeting certain expectations. If introduced in this manner, many students will sabotage their participation. If contribution is initiated, the student should get to contribute daily. The only way contribution is withdrawn is if the student is not "OK" at the time.
   c. Contribution for students can be life changing. However, it is critical that the adult community understand the "why" of contribution, otherwise it can feel like the "bad" kids are being rewarded.
      Examples of contribution:
      i. Assisting adults:
         1. Taking notes to the office;
         2. Passing out papers;
         3. Taking down chairs in the classroom.
      ii. Assisting students:
         1. Mentoring in a subject area;
         2. Providing support at recess;
         3. Helping younger students with end of the day routines.
6. Visuals

Now What?

   a. Some students will benefit from having a visual to monitor their progress. This can also be important if documentation of progress is needed to determine additional support. Finally, a visual can be a form of communication with parents in the form of a:
      i. Target behavior sheet;
      ii. Skill coaching pass;
      iii. Practice chart.

Outlasting: The Continuum of Change

To create success that goes beyond the classroom, adults must first know and understand the process of outlasting. Outlasting means providing protections, partnerships, and coaching so students can develop mastery of their missing skills. This process will take an enormous amount of time and effort. It will be a journey of moving forward and unfortunately moving backwards on occasion. There is a four-step continuum that can serve as a guide in this journey. It is not a flow chart, but rather one of milestones to be achieved. When working with student behavior, the support of a student cannot be a prescribed solution. Changing student behavior is not exact and will require different types of input. To support individual students effectively requires data. Equally important is teacher perception. Teachers know their students and what is working and not working. Their input is critical to determine the next steps. It is also important to note that this continuum can't be time based as each individual will change at a different rate and have different needs throughout the process. This continuum is fluid, meaning the student may progress or regress in spurts throughout their journey to true change. Outlasting is the most emotionally difficult, but the most positively impactful, thing we can do for students.

Outlasting is:
- Building and staying in a relationship;
- Holding students accountable;
- Natural consequences;
- Taking as long as needed;
- Being consistent;
- Working with and for the students;
- Communication with families;
- Creating and modifying a plan as needed;

- Following established structures (early intervention, caring confrontation);
- Avoiding power struggles;
- Non-emotional, concise communication;
- Giving students time to look at the problem and its impact;
- In-depth processing;
- Helping students find ways to contribute to the school;
- Firm/fair;
- Maintaining professionalism;
- Helping the students change;
- Teaching and practicing a skill.

Outlasting is *not*:
- Abandoning or rejecting the relationship;
- Being permissive;
- Punishing;
- Time-based;
- Ignoring the problem;
- Giving in;
- Changing the rules;
- Using emotion to communicate;
- Escalating the student;
- Giving answers;
- Negative, non-verbal communication.

The following is an overview of each milestone on the journey to change (refer to Appendix 2.9).

Non-compliance

When students are non-compliant, they are either overtly or covertly out of bounds. When they are overtly out of bounds it is easier for the adult community to increase restrictions since the behavior is frequently disruptive to the learning environment. However, while students who are covertly out of bounds may not be disrupting the learning of others, they are still frequently not able to follow rules or let adults be in charge. Non-compliance is driven by the frequency of behavior vs. the outrageousness of the action. In order to stop non-compliant behavior, protections/restrictions must be implemented.

Protection/restriction is the support provided to students when they are struggling to make good choices. Protections and restrictions are synonymous. They are based on what the student's repetitious behavior tells the adults they can't manage. (Some examples are listed in the Elementary and Secondary Plan for Success; see Appendices 2.8 and 2.7.) By thinking in terms of protection, it helps shift adult thinking from punishment to support. When implementing protections and increased relationships, this can become a positive intervention.

The protections put in place must be intrusive enough to stop the behavior. Being intrusive is frequently uncomfortable for adults as they are more accustomed to putting strategies in place as opposed to protections intended to stop behavior. The behavior must be stopped first before teaching a new skill. Intrusive protections will likely increase student discomfort. This discomfort is critical for change to occur. It is very typical for students to resist these protections initially. While the student experiences discomfort due to protections, it is imperative that the adults increase contact and their relationship with the student. When adults intentionally increase relationships, the student can learn to trust that they are trying to help them stay out of trouble. Students typically resist with less determination if the adults are continuing to increase relationships.

Example: A student is asked to sit in the safe seat to decrease disruptions. Often it is tempting to make this protection very temporary, but in fact to stop the behavior it requires more time.

Providing the time needed for change is an example of being intrusive enough.

Compliance

When students are compliant, they are able to adhere to the existing protections and no longer resist. However, this change in behavior is temporary as it is simply based on not liking the protections and has little to do with long-term change. If protections are reduced, the behavior is sure to return within hours to days, thus creating a need to restrict again. When protections are reinstated, there will be greater resistance from the student. So, when compliance is achieved, protections must remain in place and the adults must continue to focus on the relationship. At this point the adults should start teaching and practicing the skills the student is missing. Practice of the skill will be required to develop enough rote muscle memory to replace the original, ineffective response. Additionally, this is the time to consider having the student contribute to the community in some manner to increase confidence, belonging, empathy, significance, or skill competence.

Compliance can undermine true transformation. When student behavior stops, there is relief in the classroom and adults will frequently want to reduce protections and return to life as it was. To create long-term change, it is necessary for planning (both protections and teaching) to go beyond compliance to partnership. As acceptance progresses the adult should feel the student's effort and sincerity begin to increase. This is an indicator that the student is moving toward partnership. Compliance is doing the right thing due to external factors. However, long-term change is created by internalizing a factor.

Example: A student is moved away from the whole group due to talking during direct instruction. When the student is moved back with the group they resume talking during instruction. This demonstrates that the restrictions are what stopped the behaviors, not the student's internal skill set.

Partnership

When students are beginning to put forth as much effort as the adults, they are entering a partnership. They will begin to do the right thing due to prior success during compliance. Students start to experience internal motivation at this point. This is the indicator that true long-term change can occur. When a student is in partnership with the adults, this does not mean perfection from the student. It does, however, mean that the student is coachable and will own their behavior when they have made a mistake.

Partnership can sometimes polarize staff members since students will not partner with all adults at the same time or pace. The adults must understand how to transfer partnerships, so students are more likely to allow a greater number of adults to be in charge and coach them. During this part of the process, the adults in collaboration with the student should consider reducing protections. Traditionally, we have reduced protections too quickly and this causes the student to fail. Reducing protections is a gradual release process as the student works on utilizing their new skill. If a student fails, that does not mean that the process is not working, it simply means that the team needs to look at how to best reinstate protections, so the student does not get in trouble and is able to continue to partner with the adults.

Now What?

The process of learning a new skill and being able to utilize that skill in multiple environments takes time, support, and practice. Also, during partnership student growth can be increased if they are able to start skill coaching a peer. This is a powerful way to help students gain independence around specific skills much as occurs in the academic realm. When a student is coaching another student, they may still be receiving coaching from adults. This is not a "one or the other" process.

Example: A student does the wrong thing and the teacher redirects. When in partnership, a student will accept the redirect and be able to be honest about what went wrong without resistance.

Independence

When a student experiences consistent success without protections, or they can manage their own protections without the adult supervising the process, they are in independence. This is the final step in true long-term change. This does not mean that the student will never need support again. In fact, this is a perfect opportunity to have the student tell their success story to others in order to help them change their inner dialogue (see Dweck, 2006). Adults must continue to stay in the relationship with the student and assess how they are managing.

Intentionally Supporting Change

By using the "outlasting continuum for change" schools can identify and support students more efficiently. This continuum should be revisited monthly. Revisiting will allow adults to see progressions or regressions of students and be more responsive to their needs. It will also allow the adult community to see growth over the course of time. Additionally, it will help school communities operate more as an "Our Kids" community and that every adult is responsible for the success of every child. The outlasting continuum of change becomes the school's pacing guide regarding behavior and should be a resource in every behavior problem-solving meeting.

When embarking on the journey from non-compliance to independence it will be important that the involved adults work as a team and have parent support and communication. This process is much slower than traditional discipline and there will be many setbacks throughout the journey. It can feel like progress is not being made. Because transformation requires significant time, adults must embrace vulnerability and perseverance. Brown (2012) defines vulnerability as going into a process without knowing the outcome.

When schools have been able to support students to move from non-compliance to compliance, partnership, and eventually independence, they have contributed to a student's life change. The schools that take on life change vs. compliance begin to view difficult students not as obstacles, but as opportunities. Staff understand that as an "Our Kids" community they get to contribute to a student's increased success, not only in school but in life.

Rewards

What part do rewards play in a student's life change? Do they play a part, or are they simply manipulation? Yes, rewards play a significant role in supporting students to make change.

Rewards can be a strategy utilized when helping students stop unwanted behavior. This will allow them to move from non-compliance to compliance. However, once a student has reached compliance it will be critical to reduce rewards, enhance relationships, and teach a new skill, which will increase the student's internal motivation and their progress toward independence.

End of Chapter Reflection and Questions

- **What activities are needed to help your building team stay engaged in CAE throughout the entire school year?**
- **Referring to the Thinking Flow Chart, how will this tool help you address and support students?**
- **Do staff understand the importance of early intervention in your classroom/school?**
- **What words will you use during caring confrontation?**
- **Think of a student who needs individual support. How would you answer the four questions listed in "identifying support for individual students"?**
  - What does the student's repetitious behavior tell us they can't manage?
  - What restrictions does the student need to stop the behavior, based on what they can't manage?

- What skill do we need to teach and practice?
- How and when do we reduce restrictions?
- **Develop a lesson plan for addressing "gateway behaviors" in your classroom/in your building.**
    - Define gateway behaviors as part of a class meeting. Allow students to participate in developing a list of these behaviors.
    - Increase class understanding about why these behaviors will be addressed.
    - Teach students how the adult will address individuals when a gateway behavior occurs (either at the time or later).
    - Teach students how to respond when addressed by an adult regarding a gateway behavior.
    - Teach students what is expected if they are not able to respond correctly.

Appendix 2.1 Guide for the Development of Common Area Expectations

Now What?

Area or Time of Day	Student Procedure	Student Accountability	Adult Procedures	Adult Accountability
Arrival	What time are students allowed in the building? What is the dress code? Are students expected to adhere to the dress code? What are students expected to sound like (noise level)? How are students expected to greet staff and each other? Where are students' backpacks expected to be? What are students expected to do physically (walk, be in a line)? Are there visuals to mark which side of the hall to walk and stopping points for safety? Where are students expected to go? In what time frame are students expected to get there? How and when will students be taught the expectations and procedures?	If a student doesn't follow the procedures how will the adults intervene? What happens when students resist or defy adult intervention? What kind of restitution and planning are students responsible for? Which adult(s) will be in charge of holding students accountable? Who is responsible for sharing information about the students with parents? Who is in charge of making a plan for continually defiant and disruptive students? What kinds of restrictions and supports are available to create effective plans? How many times will students be allowed to get in trouble before supportive action is taken?	Who supervises common areas during arrival? Have problem areas been identified (bathrooms, stairwell, lockers)? Are the adults stationed in effective supervisory areas? What time does supervision start and are the adults consistently on time? Are the adults greeting and supervising students? Are the adults taking emotional temperatures? Are the adults using early intervention when procedures aren't followed? Are the adults skilled at confronting students in a direct and respectful manner? What is the exact manner of intervention? Is there a process to identify and plan for students who struggle following the procedures? Is there a plan and backup system to support adults when students don't comply?	How will an adult be held accountable within the community if one of the following issues occur (last resort answer is administration handles it? • An adult is frequently late for duty. • An adult is permissive and is not requiring students to follow the procedures. • An adult is getting angry and aggressive with students. • Struggling students are not getting the support they need. Backup and support plans are not being utilized or are not working? • Parents think the procedures are too rigid and unfair.

Now What?

Area or Time of Day	Student Procedure	Student Accountability	Adult Procedures	Adult Accountability
Breakfast	Is there a procedure for entering the cafeteria? Is there assigned seating at breakfast? Do students have to raise their hand if they need something or need to leave their seat? Do adults come to get students from the cafeteria to start the day? What is the exact dismissal procedure? When will students dump their trays? What is the expected voice volume?	Is there a safe seat in the cafeteria? What is the plan if a student cannot handle being in the cafeteria? Do adults who supervise breakfast have a way to track behavior concerns? What is the follow through if a student has a behavior problem in the cafeteria?	What time should adults arrive to supervise breakfast? Do adults have assigned supervision areas in breakfast? Is there a method to document behavior concerns? What is the system for the supervising adult to follow up with the student of concern when needed?	Same as above

(Continued)

Now What?

Area or Time of Day	Student Procedure	Student Accountability	Adult Procedures	Adult Accountability
Restrooms	Is there a procedure for restrooms at the elementary level? Is the procedure the same for each grade level at elementary? How many students are allowed in the restroom at one time? How do adults supervise both boys and girls restrooms? Has there been an assigned student restroom monitor?	What is the response if a student does not properly follow the procedures? Is there an option for individual or isolated restroom use if needed for specific students? How is that plan monitored for individual students? Are restroom breaks timed and escorted for individual students?	Is there an established plan for supervision of restrooms? Do the adults or students make sure the restroom is clean after each use? Is there an established restroom schedule so that classes do not run into each other on restroom breaks?	Same as above
	Are there procedures for handwashing? What does the rest of the class do while waiting to go into the restroom? What is the expected voice volume?			

48

Area or Time of Day	Student Procedure	Student Accountability	Adult Procedures	Adult Accountability
Lunch	Is there a specific time for each class to arrive at lunch? What is the procedure for entering the cafeteria and getting lunch? Is each class required to have a seating assignment? Do students have to be recognized to get out of their seat? Is there a procedure for students to get help when needed? What is the procedure for clean up? What is the procedure for exiting the cafeteria? What is the expected voice volume? Are there different voice volume expectations at different times? Is there a period of no talking during lunch time?	What is the plan for students who consistently struggle in the cafeteria? Is there a level system in place for students K-8 for concerns in the cafeteria? Do the high school students need a seating assignment for lunch? Does there need to be a level system for high school students for cafeteria time?	Are specific adults assigned to specific areas for supervision? Do the adults have a system to document behavior concerns during lunch? How do supervisors communicate with teachers when students struggle in the cafeteria? Is there a system in place for the supervising adults to follow up with students who have a behavior problem?	Same as above

(Continued)

Now What?

Area or Time of Day	Student Procedure	Student Accountability	Adult Procedures	Adult Accountability
	If so, how is the start of the silent period announced?			
Hallways	What are the specific procedures for students in the hallway (elementary)? Have we taught appropriate voice volume for hallways? Does elementary require no talking in hallways? Are there stopping points for students when they are transitioning in hallways? Do we require walk and talk at the high school level?		Do elementary teachers walk their students in line? Do teachers walk at about the halfway point of the line? Do teachers have a plan B if students cannot walk in line with the class? Are teachers (secondary) joining any group of students that are three or more? Does everyone verbally intervene in a common way when students misbehave in hallways?	

Area or Time of Day	Student Procedure	Student Accountability	Adult Procedures	Adult Accountability
Recess (other)	Do students know the procedure for how to use all equipment? Are there assigned play areas at recess? Is there a developed level system for students who struggle at recess? Are students allowed to change activities during recess? Do students know where and how to line up when recess is over?	When students aren't able to manage recess, how do the adults plan for them? When students have individual concerns at recess, is the student accountable to the adult in charge?	Is there a level system for recess? How is that communicated to the recess supervisors? Are parents notified if there is a recess plan? Are adults assigned specific areas to supervise at recess? Do adults have a plan if students are not able to manage at recess?	Same as above
Departure	Is there a specific procedure for students who are bus riders? Is there a specific procedure for students who are walkers? Is there a specific procedure for students who are in after school? Do students know and understand the procedures for dismissal?	Are there specific students who struggle with dismissal? Are there older students who can help younger students prepare for dismissal? Are there specific plans for students who struggle?	Do adults have assigned supervision areas during dismissal? Are we holding students who struggle in dismissal accountable the next day? Is there a plan for Accountability if problems occur during dismissal?	Same as above

(Continued)

Appendix 2.2 Elementary Teacher Classroom Management

- Preparation
  - Will you ask students to do morning work?
  - Is the schedule posted for the day?
  - Do you have all materials organized for the day in order to teach without disruption?
- Arrival
  - How do you want students to physically enter the room?
  - How do you want students to greet you?
  - How will you greet students?
  - What are the first three to five things you want students to do as soon as they enter the room?
  - What work will you have for students when they arrive?
  - What is the expected voice volume?
- Room arrangement
  - How will you arrange your room so that you can supervise all areas?
  - Where will you have carpet seating?
  - Where will you have centers?
  - Will there be areas that are off limits to students?
  - How will you designate off limit areas?
  - Where will student supplies (crayons, paper, etc.) be stored?.
  - What supplies will you have on the student desks or tables?
- Seating arrangement **(assigned seating required)**
  - Will you have students start in individual seating (rows) or group seating?
  - What boundaries will you teach them about their areas?
  - How will you create seating assignments (boy/girl, alphabetically)?
  - How frequently will you change seating assignments?
  - What will you do if students are in the wrong seats? (Other than using the BIST continuum.)
- Carpet seating assignments **(assigned seating required)**
  - How will you create seating assignments on the carpet (in a circle, rows)?
  - How will you want students to sit on the carpet (criss-cross, on pockets, personal space)?
  - How will you teach them how to sit?

- Transitions to desk
    - How will you give directions for transitions?
    - What will be the exact starting point (a "go" word, hand signal)?
    - How will you time the transition?
    - What will be the exact ending point (heads down, eyes on you)?
    - What will you do if a student does not transition within the time frame?
- Transitions to and from groups or carpet
    - What will be the procedure for students moving from seats to carpet or carpet to seats?
    - How much time will you allow for this transition?
    - How will you teach this procedure?
    - What will you do if a student does not transition within the time frame?
- Collaborative grouping
    - How will you assign groups (high/low ability, boy/girl)?
    - What will be the procedure to get into collaborative groups?
    - How will you assign roles for the group?
    - How will you give students this information?
- Hallway behaviors
    - How will you determine line order?
    - Will you have one long line or two short lines?
    - Where will you as the teacher walk in relation to the line?
    - How often will you have stopping points?
    - What will be the behavior standards for your lines (no talking, where will hands be, how close to the person in front of you)?
    - What will you do if a student does not meet this standard?
    - What will you require of students prior to getting into line?
    - What will be the procedure to get into line?
    - How will you teach this information?
    - How will you give non-verbal signals to students in the hall to redirect them?
    - Should teacher standards be different from student standards when in the line?
- Procedures
    - What procedures do you want your students to know within the classroom?

Now What?

- Sharpening pencils;
- Handing out papers;
- Handing in papers;
- Getting Kleenex;
- Disposing of trash;
- Getting teacher attention/waiting for help;
- When students are tardy or absent;
- Leaving the classroom individually;
- Getting out materials/collecting materials;
- Others?
- Restrooms
  - What will be your procedure for using the restroom in groups?
  - What will be your procedure for individual restroom breaks?
  - What will you teach students about using the restroom (washing hands, paper towels, picking up trash, horse play, voice volume)?
  - What will you do if a student does not meet the standard?
- Behavior standards **(No talking without permission/No getting out of your seat without permission)**
  - Behavior bottom line **(It is never okay to be disruptive, it is never okay to be hurtful)**.
  - How will you define hurtful and disruptive?
  - How will you teach this to students?
  - When they are not meeting the standards how will you let them know? (Other than using the BIST continuum.)
  - When you verbally intervene with students, what words will you use to address them?
  - What is your plan to get to students when you need to talk to them?
  - What will you do if they do not respond to your redirect? (Other than using the BIST continuum.)
- Ratio of positive to redirection
  - How many positives should students receive in relation to each redirect?
  - How will you provide positives to students (individually, group, verbally, socially, tangibly)?
- Learner's position
  - What do you want a student's listening position to be when giving direct instruction?

- How will you teach this to students?
- What will you do if students do not adhere to the listening position? (Other than using the BIST continuum.)
- Movement during independent work or instruction time
  - When you are instructing, can you see every student?
  - When you interact with individual students, can you see the entire class?
  - Are you moving throughout the classroom during independent work?
  - How will you assess if students are engaged in learning?
  - What will you do if a student is not engaged in learning?
- Communication with specialists
  - How will you communicate with specialists both when dropping students in specials and when picking them up?
  - What do you feel needs to be communicated?
  - What will you do if a student struggles in specials?
- Communication with parents
  - How often will you communicate with parents?
  - How many positive phone calls do you feel should be made in relation to concerning phone calls?
  - Who in your building can support you when contacting difficult parents?
- Dismissal
  - What time will the pack up procedure begin? How many minutes are needed? (Not prior to 3:35.)
  - What will be your procedure for packing up at the end of the day?
  - Will students be allowed to talk?
  - Will you have requirements about their desks, chairs, and area?
  - How will you teach them this information?
  - What will you do if a student does not stay within the boundaries?

Appendix 2.3 Secondary Teacher Classroom Management

- Preparation
  - Will you always have a bell ringer for the students to start class?
  - How much time will you allow for bell ringers?
  - Do you know in advance what work you will use for samples?
  - Do you know what the assignment for the day will be and why you are asking kids to do this assignment?
  - Do you have a timer available in your room for pacing needs?
  - How will you assess if your instructional pacing is appropriate?
- Written procedure for arrival
  - How should kids greet the teacher?
  - How should they walk in the classroom?
  - What should they do with materials?
  - What is the first activity they should do?
  - When is a student considered tardy?
- Written procedure for dismissal
  - **The bell does not dismiss students.**
  - What will be the required activity when the bell rings?
  - How will you get students to follow through on this activity?
  - Will there be any cleaning or organizing prior to dismissal?
  - Will cleaning or organizing be assigned to certain students or all students?
  - **Students who need escorts should move after the passing period.**
- Written procedure for getting into groups and back to assigned seating
  - How will you determine assigned seating?
  - How will you group students?
  - What amount of time will you give students to move from one situation to the other?
- Assign students to either groups or pairs
  - How will you assign students to groups or pairs? (High/low, same levels together, boy/girl?)
  - How quickly will you expect them to move?
  - What rules will you have when working collaboratively?
  - How will you assign roles within the group?

Now What?

- Determine bottom line behavior
    - How will you teach what the bottom line is for each activity?
    - What will you do if students don't meet the bottom line?
    - How often will you review this with students?
- Movement during instruction and independent work
    - When you are instructing, can you see every student?
    - When you interact with individual students, can you see the entire class?
    - Are you moving throughout the classroom during independent work?
    - How will you assess if students are engaged in learning?
    - What will you do if a student is not engaged in learning?
- Procedures within the classroom
    - How will you pass out information, books, etc.?
    - How will you collect papers, books, etc.?
    - How will you manage kids who do not have supplies?
    - How will you manage the process of sharpening pencils?
    - How will you manage trash needs and Kleenex?
    - What is the expectation for students to participate in discussions?
- Transitions within the classroom
    - What will be your starting signal for a transition?
    - How will you give information/steps for the transition?
    - What will be your ending point for the transition?
    - How will you make kids aware and then track the time frame for the transition?
    - What will you do if kids don't transition within the time frame?
- Confronting student behavior
    - Go to students to address individual behavior.
    - Use proximity and teacher looks as first intervention.
    - Do not sit at desk when students are in the room.
    - Are you going to teach your students about how you will redirect them?
    - What is your plan B if students do not respond to your redirect?

Appendix 2.4 Questions to Enhance Problem Solving

(To be used in grade level or team meetings on a regular basis.)

Identification
- Which students are you concerned about based on our data collection system?
- Which "goal for life" are they missing?
- Are there more problems inside the classroom, or outside the classroom?
- How does that student respond when you redirect them?
- Where is the student on the "outlasting continuum of change"?

Parents
- Have you talked to parents?
- What was their response?
- Do you feel that they can partner with the school?
- Do you need support in communication with parents?

Processing
- Have you processed with the student?
- How does the student respond?
- Can the student partner with you?
- Do things change for any amount of time after you process?

Planning
- Is this student on a "success plan"?
- What parts of the day are the hardest for this student?
- Is there a pattern to the behavior?
- Do you know what type of day it will be as soon as they enter the classroom?

Skill-based coaching
- Is the student doing skill-based coaching with anyone?
- What does skill-based coaching look like?

- What impact does skill-based coaching have on the student's behavior?
- How many times a day is he or she practicing?

Follow up
- When should we talk about this student again?
- Should we invite parents in for a conference?

Review students (student previously on plans)
- Is the student staying the same, getting better, getting worse?
- What does the data show for this student?
- Are there areas that need modification on their plan?
- Where is the student on the "outlasting continuum of change"?

Appendix 2.5 Student Questions for Planning

(Use the following bank of questions as a guide when forming questions to ask students in developing a Plan for Success.)

- How many elementary schools did you attend?
- Do you remember your kindergarten teacher (the first, second, etc.)?
- What was your best year in school and why?
- What was your worst year in school and why?
- Have you always had trouble in school?
- What type of things do you do that get you in trouble?
- When the teacher tells you to stop, do you:
  - Stop and stay stopped?
  - Stop and start again?
  - Talk back?
- Do you get in trouble more often with adults or with kids?
- Do you make better choices with kids or away from kids?
- Which of three feelings (mad, sad, worried) do you feel the most often?
- Does your mom (guardian) worry about you? On a scale from 1 to 10, if 1 is not worried at all and 10 is really worried, where would she be?
- Do you worry about your behavior? On the same scale where are you?
- On a scale from 1 to 10, if 1 = never do anything right, 10 = always do everything right, and 5 = get in trouble one time per week, where would you be?
- Where would you want to be?
- Do you think the adults are trying to help you or are mad at you?
- When you do something wrong and get caught, do you feel worse because what you did was wrong or because you got caught?
- What is the problem that the adults are worried about?
- Why do they see it as a problem?
- Why would we worry about this?
- Do you feel like the adults are on your side or against you?
- What do we do that makes you feel like we are on your side?
- What do we do that makes you feel like we are against you?
- Is there an adult that you feel, like no matter what, is on your side?

Appendix 2.6 Questions for Skills

I can be angry or upset and make good choices.
1. When you are mad, what can you say starting with "I think" or "I feel"?
2. What should your face look like?
3. What should your voice sound like?
4. Where can you go?
5. How long will it take you to get there?
6. What should it look like for you to get there?
7. When you get there, what will you do?
8. How long do you typically need to calm down?
9. How can you let the teacher know when you are calm?
10. Who is the best adult to help you with anger?

I can be OK when others are not OK. (Responding to other students.)
1. How will you stop yourself from saying or doing hurtful things?
2. When other students do things you don't like, what can you say to them starting with "I think" or "I feel?"
3. What should your voice sound like?
4. What should your face look like?
5. Where can you go if you are in the classroom?
6. Where can you go if you are in the hall or the cafeteria?
7. Who is an adult you can talk to?

I can be OK when others are not OK. (Responding to peer pressure.)
1. When other kids are making poor choices, where is the best place for you to go?
2. What words can you use if other kids want you to make poor choices?
3. What should your voice sound like?
4. Where can you go?
5. Who is the best adult for you to talk to?
6. How often should you talk to this adult about making good choices when you are around other kids?

I can be OK when others are not OK. (Responding to retaliation.)
1. What can you say when someone does something you don't like?

2. What should your voice sound like?
3. Where can you go?
4. Who's the best adult to talk to?
5. Are there specific places where the problems occur?
6. Are there specific kids with whom the problems occur?
7. If you are upset, how long do you need to calm down?
8. How many times a day should you practice the words you will use? Six or seven times?

I can be productive and follow directions even when I don't want to.
(Responding to direction from adults.)
1. What can you say when an adult asks you to do something you don't like?
2. What should your voice sound like?
3. Where can you go?
4. Who's the best adult to talk to?
5. Are there specific places where the problems occur?
6. Are there specific kids with whom the problems occur?
7. Are there certain adults with whom the problems occur?
8. If you are upset, how long do you need to calm down?
9. How many times a day should you practice the words you will use? Six or seven times?

I can be productive and follow directions even though I don't want to.
(Regarding following rules.)
1. When there are rules that you don't like, do you follow them or break them?
2. How can you follow rules even if you think they are stupid?
3. Who is the best adult to talk to about following rules?
4. How will you show that adult that you can follow the rules?
5. Where do you have the hardest time following rules?
6. When a teacher redirects you, what can you say in response?
7. How long should it take you to follow the rule after being redirected?
8. Are there students in your classes that can help you follow rules?

/ Now What?

Appendix 2.7 BIST Secondary Plan for Success

Student Name_____
Effective Date_____ Teachers/Staff
Review Date_____

Section 1. Life Skills. *Identify the life goal the student is working on.*

- I can make good choices even if I am mad.
- I can be okay even if others are not okay.
- I can do something even if I don't want to. (Or if it's hard)

Section 2. Skill-Based Coaching. *Identify coaching questions and replacement skill student is practicing.*

I can make good choices even if I am mad.	I can be okay even if others are not okay.
• When you are angry, what can you say beginning with "I think" or "I feel"? • How should your voice sound? • Where can you go? • How can you let the teacher know when you are calm?	• What can you say when someone does something you don't like? • How will you stop yourself from saying or doing hurtful things? • When others are making poor choices, where is the best place for you to go?
I can do something even if I don't want to. (or if it's hard) • What can you say when an adult asks you to do something you don't like? • How can you follow rules even if you don't like them? • How long should it take you to follow the rule after being redirected?	What replacement skill does student need to practice? How will student practice this skill? How many times a day will he/she practice? With whom will student practice?

Coaching with whom? _____ Times:
Where will student go if unable to partner or not okay?

Section 3. Accountability. *Identify restrictions the student needs to be successful at school.*

- Preferential Seating:____ Begin class in Safe Seat _____Other
- Build in proactive use of the Buddy Room daily

Now What?

- Return to Team Focus when sent out
- Hallway restrictions: ____ Delayed passing _____ Escort during passing
- Sheltered Arrival (report to a predetermined location each morning upon arrival)
- Lunch restrictions: ____ Safe Seat in cafeteria _____ Lunch in alternate room
- Bus: _____ Assigned seat _____ Target Behavior Sheet _____ Daily job
- Other (specify)

Section 4. Behavior Monitoring. *Identify 1–3 Target Behaviors to help the student reach their goal.*

- I will not touch others or others' things.
- I will stay supervised/in seat/in bounds.
- I will not talk or make noises.
- I will not say hurtful or negative remarks.
- I will let the adult tell me what to do and do it the first time.
- I will not make hurtful gestures.
- Other (specify)

Section 5. Contribution to building. *Daily job to contribute to the building/ increase sense of purpose.*

- What:_____
- When:_____
- With whom:_____

Section 6. Visuals

- Target Behavior Sheet_____
- Skill Based Coaching Pass_____
- Other_____

Student Signature:_____
Adult Signature:

Plan Review

Name_____Date_____

1. What day of the week do you tend to have your best behavior?

2. What day of the week tends to be the hardest for you regarding behavior?

3. What hour of the day is best for you regarding behavior?

4. What hour of the day is hardest for you to have good behavior?

5. What things are you doing better with?

6. What things are you still struggling with?

7. Where are you on a scale from 1 to 10 (1 is still struggling a lot, 10 is almost perfect)?

8. Using the answers from the above questions, what changes can be made to your plan to help you be more successful?

Next review date_____

Now What?

Appendix 2.8 BIST Elementary Plan for Success

Student Name _____   Date _____

Review Date _____

Teacher/Staff _____

Section 1. Goals for Life (*Identify the life goal the student is working on*).

- I can make good choices even if I am mad.
- I can be okay even if others are not okay.
- I can do something even if I don't want to. (Or if it's hard)

Section 2. Skill-Based Coaching (*Identify coaching questions and replacement skill the student is practicing*).

I can make good choices even if I am mad.	I can be okay even if others are not okay.	I can do something even if I don't want to. (Or if it's hard)	Replacement Skills
• When you are angry, what can you say beginning with "I think" or "I feel?" • How will your voice sound? • Where can you go to calm down? • What will I see to know you're calm?	• What can you say when someone says something you don't like? • How will you manage without making it worse? • Where will you go if others are making poor choices?	• What will you say when an adult asks you to do something you don't like? • What will it look like so you don't make it worse? • Where can you be productive without making it worse?	• Practice the words and place I will go when angry • Practice what I will say and do if someone is bothering me • Practice how to ask for help • Practice safe hands • Practice using kind words • Self-control
• Other: ____	• Other ____	• Other ____	• Other ____

Coaching with whom? _____ Times of Coaching?
Where will student go if unable to partner or not okay?

Section 3. Accountability (*Identify restrictions needed to protect the student*).

- Start the day in the Safe Seat Other:_____
- Build in proactive use of the Buddy Room daily.
- Hallway: ____Assigned Place ____Buddy Rm ____Focus Rm.
- Lunch: ____Assigned Place ____Focus Rm ____Other ____
- Group Work: ____Assigned Place ____Work by Adult ____Desk ____Safe Seat
- Recess:____ Coaching ____Choice of 2 activities ____Play in 1 area ____Focus Rm
- Specials: Assigned Place Sit by Adult____ Safe Seat____ Place____
- Bus: Assigned Seat Sheet____ Daily Job

Section 4. Target Behaviors (*Identify 1–3 target behaviors to help the student reach their goal*).

- I will not touch others or others' things
- I will stay supervised/in seat/in bounds.
- I will not talk or make noises.
- I will not say hurtful or negative remarks.
- I will let the adult tell me what to do and do it the first time.
- I will not make hurtful gestures
- Other (specify)_____

Section 5. Contribution (*Daily job to contribute to the building/increase sense of purpose*). Job _____ Time of Day_____ Adult _____

Section 6. Visual

- Target Behavior Sheet
- Coaching Pass
- Skills Practice Chart
- Picture of student showing desired behavior
- Other_____

Student will practice target behaviors _____ times per day
Student Signature:_____
Adult Signature:_____

Now What?

PLAN REVIEW   **Date**_____

What things are you doing better with?

What things are you still struggling with?

Where are you on a scale from 1 to 10 (1 is still struggling a lot, 10 is almost perfect)?

Appendix 2.9 Outlasting Continuum of Change

This tool should be used on a monthly basis to help teachers track students in their change from non-compliant to independence. Students should be placed on the continuum based on data as well as teacher perception. Also, this is a tool that should help support the movement of children from one grade to the next as well as from school to school. Many schools have hyper-linked the names in the continuum to the individual student plan.

Now What?

Non-compliance		Compliance		Partnership		Independence	
Student Response	**Adult Response**	**Student Response**	**Adult Response**	**Student Response**	**Adult Response**	**Student Response**	**Adult Response**
• Overt defiance • Covert defiance • Outrageous behavior • Constant disruption • "I'm not going to ___" • "I **hate** this school!" • "Everyone else does it!"	• Implement appropriate restrictions • Intentional relationship building with students.	• Good behavior when adults watch • Good behavior to avoid consequences • Sneaky behavior • "FINE, I'll do what you say because I HATE this!!" • "Stupid rules in this school!"	• Continue restrictions • Continue relationship • Teach missing skills	• Coachability • Good choices because it's the right thing to do • Let adults help • Good attitude toward adults • "I get it. The adults **are** on my side." • "I can make mistakes and let adults help."	• Progressive decrease in restrictions • Continue relationship • Continue practicing missing skills • Student starts coaching another student on missing skills	• No longer needs adults to coach on a regular basis • Can teach someone else the skills they have learned • "I can teach someone else." • "I can be okay no matter what."	• Re-entry into community • Continues to coach and practice skills

Specific actions in each category:

- **Non-compliance**: Staff should put protections in place that are restrictive enough to stop the acting out behavior.
- **Compliance**: Staff should increase their relationship with the student as well as considering contribution for the student. Contribution has five purposes: competence, confidence, empathy, significance, and belonging. When implementing contribution, the goal should drive the type of contribution.
- **Partnership**: Staff should focus on teaching the student's missing skill(s) and determine when a student is ready to become a coach of a younger student. The purpose of coaching is to move a student to independence.
- **Independence**: Staff should remain in the relationship, but the student has little to no assistance from the adults to continue to make good choices.

References

Brown, Brené, 2012. *The power of vulnerability: Teachings on authenticity, connections & courage*. Louisville, CO: Sounds True.

Dweck, Carol S., 2006. *Mindset; The new psychology of success*. New York, NY: Ballantine Books.

Mattos, Mike, Buffum, Austin and Weber, Chris, 2009. *Pyramid response to intervention: RTI, professional learning communities, and how to respond when kids don't learn*. Bloomington, IN: Solution Tree.

# BIST Logistics

BIST changed my whole philosophy about behavior. Being a former BD/ED, teacher I definitely "picked my battles." This allowed lower-level behaviors to continue and, as I learned, I was not preparing those students for higher expectations, whether that was General Education, High School, or the workplace. Once I adopted the BIST philosophy and began to see things through the lens of "If it won't work on the job, it won't work at school", students began to meet higher expectations and achieve more frequently. By letting students know that we care too much about them to allow them to keep making the same mistakes, we as a staff were able to outlast negative student behavior. Some students took longer than others. Because our staff united and supported students beyond their negative behavior, it has been life changing for many students. I could tell stories for days but will stick to my girl Ashley who was on an intense behavior plan for most of 7th grade and part of 8th grade. She successfully went on to High School, graduated on time and became a sought-after manager of McAllister's Deli! McAllister's frequently brings Ashley into stores that need to be "cleaned up."

Kim Donaho
Washington Middle School
Special Educaiton Department Chair
Springfield, IL

BIST Continuum of Logistics

Many people think of a safe seat when they think of BIST. This seat is one of the steps in the Continuum of Logistics but it is not the philosophical drive.

Yes, the safe seat serves a purpose in allowing a student to calm down or refocus and get back on track. However, without the philosophical foundation, moving a student to another seat provides no long-term benefits and frequently creates frustration for both the student and adult due to the repetition of behavior.

There are two frequent *misconceptions* about the Continuum:

1. *It is a flow chart.* The goal of the Continuum is to stop misbehavior and assist students in recovering so that learning continues. With this in mind, it is important that teachers have numerous options to stop such behavior. Not every student needs the steps of the continuum.
2. *The movement to the safe seat is considered Accountability.* True Accountability entails self-reflection, ownership of the problem, and coaching to change. This process requires interaction and guidance from adults, which is not acquired through a simple movement to a different location.

When considering the BIST Continuum of Logistics, all teachers should be aware that the movements within the continuum do not replace classroom management. The ultimate goal when redirecting student behavior is to create the least disruption to the classroom. Thus, teachers must continue to utilize tools such as proximity, teacher look, and other tried and true methods of redirection. However, by having a continuum of placements prior to a trip to the office, teachers have strategies to address behaviors that may have traditionally been ignored. When a behavior continues beyond classroom management, a teacher has options that do not have to include an office referral.

The BIST Continuum of Logistics includes six logistical steps that range from the least restrictive to the most restrictive options to stop student misbehavior:

1. Regular Seat—is a student's own seat in the classroom. The classroom expectations, procedures, and routines are designed to help the student succeed in this least restrictive environment.
2. Safe Seat—is another seat located in the learning environment and allows the student to continue to be a learner within their

community. It can be another chair in the classroom or a designated seat somewhere apart from the rest of the students. The purpose is to provide a place where the student can calm down/refocus and get back on track. The return to a student's regular seat is determined by the individual teacher and what is happening in the classroom. Additionally, it is important that a teacher's emotion does not determine how long the student stays in the safe seat. However, when a student is sent to a Safe Seat it is expected that the teacher and student will follow up to problem solve for Accountability regarding the disruptive behavior. This is important for students who are frequently out of bounds.

3. Buddy Room—is located outside of the current learning environment. It can be in a neighboring classroom or other designated room in the school (on or off grade level). The purpose is to provide an alternate location for the student to refocus and demonstrate classroom readiness. What dictates transition back to the classroom Safe Seat is calmness, directability, and the sending teacher's permission.

4. Recovery Room—is a safe place for escalated students or students who need additional assistance. However, the Recovery Room is also a location to increase proactive interactions with students. There are two types of visits to a recovery room—proactive and reactive.

   a. Proactive: When developing individual student plans, one consideration is a proactive visit to the Recovery Room to connect with an adult as well as practice the student's identified missing skill. (Refer to Appendix 3.1.) This can occur multiple times per day and should be approximately 1–3 minutes per visit. This is a critical component for a building to achieve when implementing BIST.

   b. Reactive: When students are escalated or have not been successful in a Buddy Room, they may visit the Recovery Room to de-escalate and start the process of becoming classroom ready. When this type of visit occurs, it is important that the Recovery Room has developed guidelines for students while in the room. It is also important that classroom expectations be in place and

the Recovery Room structures mirror classroom structures. The expectations often implemented in Recovery Rooms are:
i. No talking or noises;
ii. Raise your hand to get help;
iii. Stay in your seat or area;
iv. Stay on task and awake;
v. Follow the adult directive the first time.

For exit from the Recovery Room in a reactive visit, a student must be calm, directable, and able to complete some level of class work.

(Refer to Appendix 3.2.)

It is critical to note that many schools operate very effectively in the BIST philosophy without a Recovery Room and a full-time adult to supervise this room. When considering the implementation of the Recovery Room it is ideal that all staff members have had Basic BIST Training. Additionally, it is important that a Recovery Room maintains 80–85% proactive visits for the building to feel relief when working with difficult students.

5. Office—is the last step on the continuum within the school. At this point an administrator decides on next steps for the student. Even with an Office Discipline Referral (ODR), it is important that the student be accountable to the correct adult. Therefore, an ODR does not eliminate the need for the student and adult to reconnect and problem solve. The timing of this reconnection will be situation dependent.

6. Home—is the most restrictive environment because it occurs out of the school building. This decision must be made by an administrator in accordance with the district policy regarding sending a student home. It is important to consider a re-entry process for Accountability and planning when students return to school.

(Refer to the Suspension Re-entry Process on page 85.)

Whatever the "last step" is in the student's movement along this continuum, the journey back to their regular classroom seat repeats the same steps in the reverse order. The student must show compliance and willingness to follow expectations and there must be success in each location before the student can move to the next least restrictive environment. Of course, there are always exceptions. Not every student plan will include the return journey through the Continuum of Logistics. This must be based on the individual student and their needs. The "why" of having students return through the continuum is to allow each student to experience success at each step. When asking students to return through the continuum, the amount of time to be spent in each location is dependent on them.

The movements along the BIST Continuum of Logistics are done in a protective manner instead of being punitive in nature. This means students are redirected by an adult in a quick, kind, calm, firm, and close manner instead of an emotional or angry manner. Emotional redirects can erode the relationship and increase student resistance. The goal is to identify repetitive students and increase their individual support.

This continuum is *not* a flow chart. Not every student will follow the steps of these logistics in order. The most important answer, when asked what is next, is "It depends." This forces the adult community to begin to look at students individually. This is the ultimate goal when student behavior has gone beyond the teacher's classroom management.

The key is to move a student on the Continuum of Logistics to the *least restrictive* place, where the acting out stops.

When setting up classroom procedures a goal is to have every student in the class practice going to the Safe Seat at least one time in the first week of school (elementary classrooms). This reinforces that the Safe Seat is a classroom procedure not a punishment. Teachers should determine the procedure of how students take their materials to the Safe Seat. They may choose for them to take their materials at the time of the movement or get the materials delivered to them momentarily by the teacher or a student helper.

Here are some general guidelines about logistical movements:

Safe Seat
- High school/middle school
  - If a student is moved to the Safe Seat during a class period, the student will typically remain there for the rest of the hour. If the student behavior has been in bounds during that time, they will move to the next class. The teacher and student need to follow up with processing before that hour the next day.

- Elementary
  - If a student is moved to a Safe Seat, the student typically stays throughout the rest of that activity and may remain longer if the teacher does not have the opportunity to process with the student or the student is not emotionally ready to process. If the student remains beyond the initial activity, it is the adult's responsibility to stay in contact with the student at least one time per activity. This contact is simply to keep the relationship intact. This is not processing.

Buddy Room
- Develop a system regarding how to direct students safely to the Buddy Room. Considerations should include:
  - A method of adult communication to ensure that the student goes to the directed area;
  - Pre-assigned Buddy Rooms so that teachers know where a student will go at that moment;
  - A strategy to provide work for the student in the Buddy Room.
- The Buddy Room teacher:
  - Ensures that the arriving student is not disruptive to their classroom.
  - Does not process with the visiting student.
  - May interact with the student to keep them on track or answer appropriate questions.
  - Uses Early Intervention when needed.
  - Moves a student if they become disruptive. Movement may be to either the Recovery Room (if available) or to the Office as part of the BIST Continuum.
- High school/middle school
  - Typically, a student will stay in a Buddy Room for the remainder of that class period.
- Elementary
  - The sending teacher makes the decision when a student returns to the Safe Seat in the classroom. This is individually based.

Think Sheets

There are many examples of think sheets. (Refer to examples in Appendix 3.3.) Think sheets are not used as punishment but as an opportunity for students to reflect on their behavior. They can also be a support when processing with teachers. In addition, a think sheet can be used as a form of documentation in the student's handwriting. The use of a think sheet in the Safe Seat should be a teacher decision based on the student and the situation. The think sheet is more commonly used when the student leaves the classroom for the Buddy Room or Recovery Room, not only as a student reflection, but also as a form of adult communication.

Documenting Student Movement

As much as teacher's hate to hear this part, data keeping is an important component to effectively support students who struggle. Ideally, when a student has moved within the BIST Continuum of Logistics (including the Safe Seat) three or more times within a month, it is time to ensure that the correct supports are in place for that student.

In tracking student movements, data to be collected should include:

- Location of the movement (Safe Seat/Buddy Room/Recovery Room);
- Time of day;
- Subject area;
- Missing skills;
- Specials, lunch, and recess (elementary).

The information collected in the tracking system should be reviewed on a weekly basis. This process is most effectively done in a grade level or team meeting. The early identification allows teams to plan for students individually in a manner that stops the misbehavior and increases success. (Refer to Appendix 3.5).

Processing

The journey to accountability is just that: a journey. It is time consuming and takes practice on the part of the adult. However, it may be one of the most important aspects in supporting a student through the process from non-compliance to independence. The road to Accountability is through processing.

The processing conversation is about how students are held accountable and problem solve their mistakes. After an event happens, and the student and/or teacher are no longer emotional, it is time to talk with the student. This may require postponing the conversation until the adult has a few minutes to focus solely on the student. There are two goals when processing with a student after an event. One is to reconnect the relationship. The second is to guide the student through the problem-solving process in order to recognize the impact of their behavior and develop solutions. The learning curve for adults is moving from lecture to questions, which increases student thinking and ownership. Lecturing will not be productive in the journey to Accountability.

Things to do:
- Listen for the skill they did not use;
- Validate their feelings, not their behaviors;
- De-escalate and ask questions;
- Plan for the missing skill;
- Use conversational format to decrease tension.

Things to avoid:
- Give the students the answers—they KNOW what they did.
- Be angry or frustrated—humans mirror emotion.
- Use sarcasm—never productive with students.
- Lecture students—gives students the opportunity to increase resistance.

A one-page summary of processing, "Processing with Students," can be found in Appendix 3.4. This provides a list of the ten steps with questions to assist at each step. Table 3.1 clarifies how the ten steps coordinate with the five levels of Accountability. The "big rocks" of Accountability and the levels of Accountability were mentioned in Chapter 1. This is the philosophical drive that must be included when guiding students through Accountability. Listed in this section are the steps of processing and the purpose of each step. These are the actions that are driven by philosophical thinking.

Table 3.1 Ten Steps of Processing and the Purpose

Big Rocks of Accountability	Five Levels of Accountability	Ten Steps of Processing	Purpose of Each Step in Processing
Ownership	I did it	1. Build a relationship	Determine student's emotional level
		2. Find out what happened	Identify behavior and honesty
Partnership	I'm sorry	3. Identify the missing skill	Moves from classroom to life impact
	It's part of a problem in my life	4. Validate or empathize	Pulls student into conversation
		5. Connect the feeling to the behavior	Identifies that there is a feeling *and* a behavior
		6. Help student see it as a problem in their life	Helps the student recognize that the pattern of their behavior is hindering their success
Coachability	I accept consequences	7. Set a goal	Extend our partnership
	I accept and need help	8. Plan for the missing skill	Help student have power to use their words to get needs met
		9. Practice	Create new, effective, rote muscle memory
		10. Apology	Reconnect to community

Team Focus (Long-Term Recovery Process)

Many schools have students who display behavior that feels impossible to support. Frequently, the question teachers have is "How can we support this student while continuing the learning for others?" Initially, there must be a comprehensive understanding that continued misbehavior is driven by a missing skill. When this belief is intact, staff can teach the missing skill in order to increase the student's success (teaching). However, to achieve teaching a new life skill the acting out behavior must be stopped (protecting). This is done through putting intrusive restrictions in place and increasing the relationship with the student. In many cases, struggling students are academically behind due to their acting out behavior. They frequently have the intellectual ability to learn if the behavior can be stopped and the new skill taught and practiced. If a student does not respond to common area expectations, classroom management, and an individual plan, team focus or long-term recovery may be a valid option. This section will provide detailed guidelines of how to develop the team focus process.

It is highly suggested if a school is developing a team focus process for a student, they collaborate with colleagues, administrators, and parents. This process must also be developed within the school/district guidelines of the multi-tiered support system.

Team focus is used to protect the learning in the classroom as well as to *protect* the student from continued acting out and *teach* skills to cope with the situation leading to acting out. This requires a location in which to protect the misbehaving student. *It is not to be used as punishment* nor for *incomplete work*. While incomplete work is a serious concern, correction of that problem is not through the BIST Continuum of Logistics.

Criteria for Placement

Team focus is used when a student is unable to follow adult directions to stop behavior that is:

- Consistently hurtful, threatening, or disrespectful;
- Consistently disruptive to the learning of others.

Considerations:
- Administrators must be a part of the planning for students to enter team focus.
- Parents *must* be aware of the process and be willing to support the school.
- Teachers must be willing to stay in the relationship with the student.
- Special education students must continue to receive appropriate minutes as directed by their individualized education plan. The case manager *must* be a part of this planning. This process could be considered a change of placement and therefore may not be an appropriate strategy.

Setting up team focus:
- The student will stay with one teacher, such as math, all day long (except during that teacher's plan time). During plan time the student may go to another room or the Recovery Room if available.
- Placement of the student during team focus is based on individual needs. Schools may try to make team focus the same for each student, but it will be critical that the planning process and decision making be based on the needs of each student. Considerations:
    - Partnership with specific teacher;
    - Prior relationship with specific teacher;
    - Struggles with a specific subject area.
- Teachers have a schedule to touch base with the student daily.
- Teachers provide work for the student that is appropriate for that student's skill level.
- A plan for teaching academics must be developed.
- A plan for teaching and practicing the new skill (Refer to Appendix 3.1.)
- Team focus teacher tracks target behaviors with the student on the team focus target behavior sheet (See Appendix 3.6.)

Time frame:
- Team and/or elective teachers will determine time parameters to consider student progress. (Example: reconvene to consider progress after three days.)
- Students must meet predetermined, *reasonable* expectations. (Ideally, the student would meet 80–90% of the team focus target behavior sheet.)
- Team focus is *not* time based but is measured by student readiness and student partnership with adults.

What students will do in team focus:
- Students are housed in the Safe Seat in the team focus room and do not participate in class activities.
- Students complete work that is provided by team/electives. Students follow their current schedule for order of assignments.
- Students will need planned breaks throughout the day (determined individually).
- Students do not participate in passing periods.
- If needed, the student can participate in daily contributions.
- Students will have an assigned area for lunch.

Criteria students should meet prior to exit:
- Meet expectations (team focus target behavior sheet).
- Participate in accountability process:
  - Problem solve and make restitution based on previous problems;
  - Partner with adults, defined in the Outlasting Continuum of Change (Refer to Appendix 3.7);
  - Plan to prevent the problem from happening again.
- Complete provided work (must be determined for each student).
- Participate in the reintegration plan.

Reintegration back to regular schedule:
- Must be determined based on the individual student.
- Participate in the accountability process (listed above) and partner with adult(s) prior to reintegration.
- Reintegration is based on the student meeting their goals on the team focus target behavior sheet.
- Example of reintegration:
  - Monday student attends math and is in team focus for remainder of day (successfully).
  - Tuesday student attends math and English Language Arts (ELA) and is in team focus for remainder of day (successfully).
  - Wednesday student attends math, ELA, and social studies and is in team focus for remainder of day (struggles in social studies).
  - Thursday student attends math and ELA and is in team focus for remainder of day (successfully).

- Friday student attends math, ELA, and social studies and is in team focus for remainder of day (successfully).
- Monday student attends math, ELA, social studies, and science and is in team focus for remainder of day (successfully).
- Tuesday student attends math, ELA, social studies, science, and art and is in team focus for remainder of day (struggled in math).
- Wednesday student attends ELA, social studies, science, and art and is in team focus for remainder of day (successfully).
- Thursday student attends math, ELA, social studies, science, and art and is in team focus for the remainder of the day (successfully).
- Friday student attends math, ELA, social studies, science, art, and band (successfully).
- Monday student is back in regular schedule for entire day.
- The pace of reintegration must be determined for each student.
- The selection of classes during reintegration ideally includes student input.
- It cannot be stressed enough that this process must be developed individually for each student and the administrator must be involved in the development.
- Students will need an ongoing plan of support that will include continued protections and skill based coaching.

If problem repeats once student is out of team focus:
- The problem will likely reoccur. This does not mean that team focus did not work, it simply means that the student does not have complete mastery of the new skill.
- When this occurs, a student may need a day of team focus to get back on track. This does not mean that the student must go through the entire reintegration process. It may also be necessary to look at ongoing protections to increase success. (Examples: delayed passing period, preferred seating.)

Critical components for team focus:
- Parents, students, and administrators must be informed, prior to starting team focus.
- Details of the plan are in place.

- Schedule and document daily visits with classroom teachers. (This may require assistance by staff to cover classrooms so that teachers can visit with the student.)
- Agenda/schedule for daily assignments is provided, modified for independent work level.
- Daily target behavior sheets are filled out (see Appendix 3.6).
- Daily review of expectations with students.
- Schedule review of student progress, at a minimum weekly, as a team, then update principal and parent.
- Plan for reintegration when the student meets expectations.

Suspension Re-entry Process

There will be times when an administrator must make the decision to suspend a student. This decision is based on the school policy and the individual situation. As previously discussed, suspension does not typically change the behavior of the individual student, but rather helps set bottom line behaviors for a school. In order to reduce recidivism or repetition of suspensions, schools should consider a re-entry from the suspension process. Most schools have some type of re-entry process but often this traditional process omits student accountability and simply reiterates the expectations the student did not meet. The purpose of the re-entry process is to:

- Reconnect the student with the adults prior to interaction with other students;
- Allow the student to make up work;
- Help the student be accountable for the prior misbehavior;
- Partner with the student to create a plan to prevent the behavior from recurring.

To include reconnection and student accountability to this process, here are five considerations, both at the time of suspension and upon the student's return to school:

1. At the time of suspension, the administrator *must* contact the parent to obtain permission to bring the student back through the re-entry process. The conversation might sound like:

"We are going to suspend your daughter for _____. It would typically be a three-day suspension but if you allow her to go through the re-entry process, we will reduce the time of suspension to two days. While in the re-entry process, we will ask her to make up work, own the problem she created, process through the event and create a plan to prevent it from happening again."
2. Where will the student be housed during the re-entry process? This is frequently done with a classroom teacher as opposed to an in-school suspension area. The purpose is to help reconnect the student to the adults with whom they have relationships.
3. What work is expected from the student during the re-entry process? This must be an individual decision based on the student's ability to produce work.
4. With whom should the student process? This is to place accountability with the adult where the behavior occurred.
5. Which adults will be involved in the creation of the prevention plan? Adults closest to the situation are involved in creating the individually based plan.

The time frame for re-entry is typically one day. However, if the student is not able to meet the standards, the time may be extended. If the time is extended it is critical to communicate with parents.

Prevention

Ideally, a school should attempt to operate at 70% prevention, which means every two out of three interactions regarding behavior are prevention/proactive based. To achieve this goal, there are three levels of prevention that must be in place.

The first level of prevention was addressed in Common Area Expectations. When supervising students in common areas, all adults must be aware of the specific expectations, so when students are out of procedure they can be addressed in a predictable manner. The goal of vigilant supervision is to prevent misbehavior from occurring.

The second level of prevention is at the classroom door. This method of greeting "using the student's name has proven to have the potential to increase engagement by up to 20%, as well as decrease disruptive behavior by 9 percentage points—potentially adding an hour of engagement each day" (www.edutopia.org/article/welcoming-students-smile/). Additionally, this intentional greeting allows adults to assess students emotionally. When students are emotional, they are less receptive to learning. Therefore, teachers should have a:

1. Formalized method of greeting students;
2. Method of assessing student emotion as they enter the classroom;
3. Plan to address individual students when needed.

The third level of prevention is skill-based coaching of individual students. This is a method of preparing students for specific, appropriate actions prior to participating in a difficult task or situation.

Skill-Based Coaching

With the ever-increasing percentage of students from chaos and often trauma, teachers are left wondering, "Can I actually impact this student?" The answer in most cases is emphatically "YES!" Teachers are experts in identifying missing academic skills and being able to teach that specific skill. Behavior is comparable in the fact that it is skill based. Thus, teachers must understand how to identify a missing life skill based on the student's pattern of behavior and then how to teach that skill.

The five critical components of teaching a new life skill are:

1. Timing—when to say what you have to say;
2. Exact words—what words will be used for positive impact;
3. Tone of voice—what will the tone be to increase receptiveness;
4. Body language—how to present non-verbally in a way to be heard;
5. Proximity—where to go when emotions escalate.

By teaching these components and then practicing to mastery, students learn to use their words to express their needs as opposed to using inappropriate behavior.

Skill-based coaching is a proactive measure that, over time, has the potential to reduce behavioral concerns and facilitate real change. Once the missing skill has been identified and then taught through the above five components, coaching can begin. When providing skill-based coaching it is most effective when done through questions (Refer to Appendix 3.1.) This practice allows students to use their exact words and tone of voice in an appropriate manner. The practice will feel tedious and repetitive to adults but is what allows the development of rote muscle memory for the student. Skill-based coaching should take two minutes or less and is predictably the same each time. This method can be compared to helping athletes gain increased competence of fundamental skills for a game. The practice is done with lack of emotion and lack of distraction so the student can begin to put the skill in place when there is increased emotion or chaos. This practice remains one of the most effective, practical tools to put in place for students.

How this looks will vary for each individual student. Some students may only need skill-based coaching before a specific part of the day; other students may need more frequent coaching. To determine the needs, adults must continue to look at each child individually and make a coaching plan that is appropriate for that student.

Some students may require one adult as a coach, other students can manage multiple coaches. Certainly, classroom teachers will play a significant role in this, but as a school community look for all meaningful adult connections and utilize those connections to proactively coach students.

Example: when a student is finished eating breakfast, the cafeteria supervisor does the skill-based coaching with the student. "When your teacher asks you to do something you don't want to do, what are you going to do?" "I will say yes and do it the first time." The cafeteria employee says, "That is perfect, I will check in with you at lunch."

Students Coaching Students

Students coaching students is not a new concept. Teachers have done this for years in the academic world. As students move from partnership to independence (Outlasting Continuum of Change) they can begin to coach other students in the skill they are developing. This practice holds tremendous power for growth. The students who are receiving coaching should be at the compliance level. Allowing students to coach other students solidifies the internalization of their new skill. This process should be:

- Supervised by adults;
- Based on the concept of skill-based coaching;
- Take approximately two minutes or less;
- Occur 2–3 times per day.

End of Chapter Reflection and Questions

- **What location will be utilized as a safe seat in your classroom?**
- **Using the one-page "processing with students," practice the process out loud with a colleague.**
- **Using Appendix 3.1, develop 3–5 questions that could be used with a student that was most challenging in your classroom.**
- **What times during your day could you incorporate skill-based coaching?**

Appendix 3.1 Questions for Skill-Based Coaching

The purpose of this resource is to provide sample questions that can be used for skill-based coaching. Certainly, these are not all of the questions that might exist for coaching students. There are choices provided with some questions to provide ideas of what choice-based questions might look like. The choices provided may not be appropriate for all settings and ages. However, when choices are provided for students, it expedites the conversation and provides ideas of answers for students. Open-ended questions can lead to long pauses, striving for what adults want to hear, and manipulation. Use as is appropriate for each individual student.

Skill #1: I can be angry, upset or have an overwhelming feeling without getting in trouble
- If you are angry or upset, what can you say? ("I feel angry" or "I hate this school")
- If you are angry or upset what will your voice sound like? (Angry or calm)
- What should your face look like if you are angry or upset? (Angry or calm)
- Where in the classroom can you go if you are angry or upset? (Safe Seat or reading table)
- How will you get there? (Quickly or slowly)
- When you get there, will you sit down like a student or throw yourself down?
- How long do you need to calm down: minutes, hours, or days?
- When you are calm what will we see? (Listening or not listening; working or not working)
- If you feel overwhelmed or anxious, what will we want you to say? ("I need a minute" or "This is stupid")
- If you feel overwhelmed or anxious, where can you go? (Safe Seat or reading table)
- If you feel overwhelmed or anxious, how should you move there? (Quickly or slowly)

Skill #2: I can be okay when others are not okay (retaliation)
- If someone says or does something you don't like, how can you respond? ("STOP!" or "Please don't say that")
- If someone says or does something you don't like, what will your voice sound like when you respond? (Calm or angry)

- If someone says or does something you don't like, which place in the classroom can you go? (Safe Seat or reading table)
- If someone says or does something you don't like, which adult can you tell?
- What will it look like to tell an adult if someone says or does something you don't like?

Skill #2: I can be okay when others are not okay (peer pressure)
- If someone does something that is not okay, what can you say inside your head to stay out of the situation? ("Make good choices" or "I'll do that too")
- If someone does something that is not okay, how can you keep yourself out of the situation? (Move away, put your head down)
- If you move away, where can you go? (Safe Seat, closer to the teacher)
- Which adult can you tell if others are making poor choices?

Skill #3: I can do something even if I don't want to or it is hard (rules)
- If there is a rule you don't like, what can you do? (Follow the rule or break it)
- What can you say inside your head if there is a rule you want to break? ("I should stop and make good choices" or "I don't have to follow the rules")
- Where can you go if there is a rule that is hard to follow? (Safe Seat or move away from others)
- Who is the best adult to coach you on following rules?

Skill #3: I can do something even when I don't want to, or it is hard (adult directives)
- If a teacher says something you don't like, what can you say in response? ("I hate this", "This is hard", "I need a minute")
- If you say "This is hard" or "I need a minute" what should your voice sound like? (Calm or angry)
- If you say, "I need a minute" will the adult say "Ok, you don't have to do it"? Or "Take a minute, but you still have to do it."?

Letting Adults Be in Charge

- What is it going to look/sound like for the teacher to be in charge?
    - How will your body look?
    - What will your eyes be doing?
    - Will you be sitting or standing?

BIST Logistics

- If you can't let the teacher be in charge, what do you think will happen?
- Can you let the teacher be in charge today even though it's hard?
- What will be the sign, or how will you let me know, that you're not going to be okay?
- How long/how much time should I allow for you to follow my directions?
- Is there any way I can help you follow directions?

What to Do When Kids Can't Let Adults Be in Charge

- How can you let the teacher be in charge?
    - How will your body look?
    - What will your eyes be doing?
    - Will you be sitting or standing?
- What are your actions when a teacher gives directions?
- What are you going to do when a teacher asks you to do something you don't want to?
- When is it okay not to follow the adult's directions?
- What do you think will happen if you're not able to let the adult be in charge?
- How does your body react when the teacher asks you to do something you don't want to do? What will you do when you feel that way?

Questions for Unstructured Areas

- **Recess**
    - What are you going to do if someone ___ you? (Cuts in line, kicks, pushes, throws rocks, doesn't follow game rules)
    - What does it look like when the whistle blows?
    - What does it look like when you come into the building?
- **Cafeteria**
    - How can you have a good lunch period?
    - What does it look like when you're standing in line?
    - What does it look like when you're sitting at the table?
    - What are you going to do when you're finished eating?
    - How will you ask for something you need?

- **Restroom**
    - How are you going to act with others in the restroom?
    - What should your voice sound like in the restroom?
    - What are you going to do when others bother you in the restroom?
- **Hallways**
    - What does it look like to walk in the hall?
    - What should your voice sound like in the hallway?
    - How long should it take you to get to your next location?

Questions for Impulse Control

- What will it look like ...?
- What will it sound like ...?
- What does it feel like ...?
- When can you ...?
- What are some ways you ...?
- Can you show me ...?

Anger Management

- On a scale of 1–5, where are you on the anger meter?
- What makes you angry?
- How will you handle the situation?
- What words will you use if you get angry? ("I" statements)
- What does it look like when you handle your anger successfully?

What Does It Look Like to Be at School?

- Show me how you're going to sit at circle time.
- Show me what your hands will be doing at circle time.
- Tell me what you are going to do when the clean-up bell rings.
- Show me how it looks to raise your hand to tell the teacher something.
- Show me how your body looks when you are in line.

BIST Logistics

- Show me how your body walks down the hall or sidewalk.
- Show me how your body will wait in line to use the sink, get a drink, use the bathroom, get your lunch tray.
- Show me how your body will look when you are at the table waiting for a snack.
- Show me how your body will look when you are waiting for your ride home.

Organization

- What are you going to need to get your day started?
- What can you do if you don't have a supply that you need?
- Is your homework complete and with you? (In your binder?)
- Classroom check-in: On a scale of 1–5 how would you rate yourself? (1 no organization (the dog ate my homework); 5 very organized)
- Are you more organized at home or at school?
- What does it look and feel like to be organized?
- What are some things that keep you from being prepared?

Kids that Won't Work (Teachers that Do)

- What do you need to know in order to complete the assignment?
- How will you react (or look) if you need help?
- What will the result be if you do not complete your work?
- Do you understand why you are being asked to do this? Please explain, elaborate, tell me more.
- What are your educational goals?
- What does success look like to you?
- Do you have a place to complete homework?
- Do you know how to get help with your work?
- Do you have the materials that are required to complete your assignments?
- How much sleep have you had this week?
- When have you experienced academic success?
- How will you feel when you have completed this assignment? (Carefully and thoughtfully)
- How can we make this assignment fit your learning style?

Appendix 3.2 Logistics Continuum

Expectations Safe Seat

Adult Expectations	Student Expectations
• Designate Safe Seat within the classroom. • Teach, practice, and role play with students what it looks and sounds like to move to the Safe Seat. • Teach and practice with students how to complete a think sheet appropriately. • Provide work and/or think sheets while student is in the Safe Seat. • Make contact with the student within 30 minutes. • When student is ready, process and plan. • If student is not ready to process, but meeting the standard, student remains in Safe Seat. • If student is disruptive or hurtful in the Safe Seat, utilize placement continuum.	• Walk to the Safe Seat quietly. • Stay in seat/area. • Complete think sheet appropriately. • Begin and/or complete assignments as given. • Demonstrate ability and readiness to process. • Partner, practice, and plan with the adult.

BIST Logistics

Buddy Room

Adult Expectations	Student Expectations

• Establish designated Buddy Room and alternate.
• Teach expectations and practice with students up front:
  • How to arrive
  • Where to go
  • What it looks like to sit in the Buddy Room and meet expectations
  • What can be worked on while in the Buddy Room
  • How to ask for help
• Communicate with receiving teacher the Buddy Room expectations.
• Designate Buddy Room seat within the class.
• Look at think sheet to see if there is a designated time for student to return to the classroom.
• Continue to teach your class.
• If student is disruptive or hurtful, utilize placement continuum.
	• Walk to Buddy Room quietly.
	• Stay in seat/area.
	• Complete think sheet and/or designated work.
	• Demonstrate ability and/or readiness to process.
	• Process, partner, and plan with adult where the issue first occurred. (At the secondary level, make appointment to process with the teacher and follow through.)

Recovery Room

Adult Expectations	Student Expectations
• Send recovery pass as soon as possible • When student initially enters recovery, contact with the sending teacher should be made within 30–45 minutes. • Maintain contact 3–4 times a day. • Send work for the student. • Process, practice, and plan with the student. • Discuss student working their way back through the continuum.	• Sit where adult asks you to sit. • Allow the adult to assist you in calming down. • Complete think sheet. • Begin classroom assignments. • Develop plan and apology for reintegration into the classroom. • Practice the new skill. • Process, apologize, and plan with the classroom teacher.

Team Focus (Secondary)

Adult Expectations	Student Expectations
• Bring student into team time. • Discuss with student the problems that he or she is experiencing. • Discuss intent of team focus with the student. • Discuss target behaviors and what it will look like (% of target) to reintegrate back into class. • Arrange for student to remain and work in one classroom. • Inform all staff working with student (including attendance secretary). • Arrange for classroom work to be provided for student (including specials, exploratory teachers). • Arrange for supervision when teacher/class has lunch. • Schedule daily visits from the classroom teachers. • Arrange skill based coaching at arrival and departure to build and maintain relationship. • Discuss expectations and review progress of target behaviors. • Review and discuss reintegration schedule. • If student is unable to maintain standard in team focus, utilize placement continuum.	• Partner and discuss issues with team. • Identify target behavior(s) to work on. • Allow teachers to tell you what room you will be in during the school day. • Demonstrate the ability to work on assignments. • Comply with adult requests the first time. • Partner and plan during skill based coaching. • Participate in discussion of reintegration schedule.

Appendix 3.3 Example Think Sheets

Think Sheet

Name _____
Date _____

Goals For Life

_____I can make good choices even if I am mad.
_____I can be okay even if others are not okay.
_____I can do something even if I don't want to. (Or if it's hard)

Word Box			
mad	hit	listen	teacher
students	sad	argued	work

Draw what happened, then write a sentence about it.

Draw how that made you feel, then write a sentence about it.

BIST Logistics

Draw what you did that was a problem, and then write a sentence about it.

Draw what you can do next time that won't cause a problem, and then write a sentence about it.

Draw a picture of the people that can help you, and then write a sentence telling how they can help.

Adult signature _____ Student signature _____

BIST Logistics

Think Sheet

Name _____   Date _____

_____ I can make good choices even if I am mad.
_____ I can be okay even if others are not okay.
_____ I can do something even if I don't want to. (Or if it's hard)

- What did you do?

_____

- What problem did it cause?

_____

- What can you do to resolve it?

_____

- What can you do to keep this from happening again?

_____

BIST Logistics

Think Sheet

Name: _____ Date: _____

1 What happened?

2 What problem did this cause?

3 What will I do to fix it?

4 What is my plan to keep this problem from happening again?

BIST Logistics

Appendix 3.4 Processing with Students

1. Build a relationship
    a. Start with a question about how they are doing.
2. Find out what happened
    a. *Why did I send you to the safe seat?*
    b. *What happened?*
    c. *What did I see?*
3. Identify missing skill
    a. The adult does this—in your head
        i. I can make good choices even if I am mad.
        ii. I can be okay even if others are not okay.
        iii. I can do something even if I don't want to. (Or if it's hard)
4. Validate or empathize
    a. Kids have to know that we hear them before they will listen to us.
5. Connect the feeling to the behavior
    a. *When you were mad what did you do?*
    b. *When you didn't like what the teacher said what did you do?*
    c. *When other kids were making poor choices what did you do?*
6. Help students see it as a problem in their lives
    a. *Do you always get in trouble when you are mad?* (Skill #1)
    b. *When other kids make poor choices, do you make good choices or poor choices?* (Skill #2)
    c. *When other kids do things you don't like do you get in trouble?* (Skill #2)
    d. *When there are rules you don't like, do you follow them or break them?* (Skill #3)
    e. *When an adult says something you don't like, do you make things better or worse?* (Skill #3)
7. Set the goal
    a. Extend a partnership
        i. *I don't want you to be in trouble just because you're mad—can you let me help you?*
        ii. *I don't want you to be in trouble just because you don't like what the adult says—can you let me help you?*

8. Plan
    a. Use the questions for skills to develop a new skill set
        i. Timing
        ii. Exact words
        iii. Tone of voice
        iv. Body language
        v. Proximity
        vi. Intention
9. Practice
    a. Plan how and when to practice
10. Apologize
    a. *I'm sorry for…*
    b. *Next time I will…*
    c. *Can you accept my apology?*

Appendix 3.5 BIST Tracking Sheet

Elementary

Teacher Name _____

Skill 1 – I can make good choices even if I am mad.
Skill 2 – I can be okay even if others are not okay.
Skill 3 – I can do something even if I don't want to. (Or if it's hard)

Date	Student Name	Time	Safe Seat	Buddy Room	Recovery Room	Think Sheet	Processed/ Date	Skill 1,2,3	Parent Contact

Secondary

Skill 1 – I can make good choices even if I am mad.
Skill 2 – I can be okay even if others are not okay.
Skill 3 – I can do something even if I don't want to. (Or if it's hard)

BIST Logistics

Grade	Name	Date	Hour	Safe Seat	Buddy Room	Recovery Room	Think Sheet	Processed/ Date	Skill 1,2,3	Parent Contact

Appendix 3.6 Team Focus Target Behavior Sheet

Name

Date _____

Percentage Goal ____% Today's Total ____

/____ = ____%

Schedule										
No talking out or making noise.	2	2	2	2	2	2	2	2	2	2
	1	1	1	1	1	1	1	1	1	1
	0	0	0	0	0	0	0	0	0	0
Stay in seat or area.	2	2	2	2	2	2	2	2	2	2
	1	1	1	1	1	1	1	1	1	1
	0	0	0	0	0	0	0	0	0	0
Stay on task and awake.	2	2	2	2	2	2	2	2	2	2
	1	1	1	1	1	1	1	1	1	1
	0	0	0	0	0	0	0	0	0	0
Let the teacher tell me what to do the first time.	2	2	2	2	2	2	2	2	2	2
	1	1	1	1	1	1	1	1	1	1
	0	0	0	0	0	0	0	0	0	0
Raise hand to get help	2	2	2	2	2	2	2	2	2	2
	1	1	1	1	1	1	1	1	1	1
	0	0	0	0	0	0	0	0	0	0
Totals										

2—No problems, 1—responded to redirect, 0—had to move

Appendix 3.7 Outlasting Continuum of Change

This tool should be used on a monthly basis to help teachers track students in their change from non-compliant to independence. Students should be placed in the continuum based on data as well as teacher perception. Also, this is a tool that should help support the movement of children from one grade to the next as well as from school to school. Many schools have hyper-linked the names in the continuum to the individual student plan.

Non-compliance			Compliance		Partnership	Independence	
Protection			Teaching				
Student Response	Adult Response	Student Response	Adult Response	Student Response	Adult Response	Student Response	Adult Response
• Overt defiance • Covert defiance • Outrageous behavior • Constant disruption • "I'm not going to." • "I **hate** this school!!" • "Everyone else does it!"	• Implement appropriate restrictions • Intentional relationship building with students	• Good behavior when adults watch • Good behavior to avoid consequences • Sneaky behavior • "FINE, I'll do what you say because I HATE this!" • "Stupid rules in this school!"	• Continue restrictions • Continue relationship • Teach missing skills	• Coachability • Good choices because it's the right thing to do • Let adults help • Good attitude toward adults • "I get it. The adults **are** on my side." • "I can make mistakes and let adults help."	• Progressive decrease in restrictions • Continue relationship • Teach missing skills	• No longer need adults to coach on a regular basis • Can teach someone else the skills they have learned • "I can teach someone else." • "I can be okay no matter what."	• Re-entry into community • Continues to coach and practice skills

Specific actions in each category:

- **Non-compliance**: Staff should put protections in place that are restrictive enough to stop the acting out behavior.
- **Compliance**: Staff should increase their relationship with the student as well as consider contribution for the student. Contribution has five purposes: competence, confidence, empathy, significance, and belonging. When implementing contribution, the goal should drive the type of contribution.
- **Partnership**: Staff should focus on teaching the student's missing skill(s) and determine when a student is ready to become a coach of a younger student. The purpose of coaching is to move a student to independence.
- **Independence**: The staff should stay in the relationship, but the student has little to no assistance from the adults to continue to make good choices.

"Our Kids" Community

> BIST has given our school community a united "why." We want every child who enters our building to experience success. In order for student success to occur, all adults must view every child as their obligation. The biggest change has been the consistency at the adult level both in the common areas and the classrooms. All adults respond to behaviors in the same way, with common language, creating predictability for students, and increasing the level of trust among adults. Thus, our entire school climate has become more positive and supportive. Teachers are given layers of support to provide students with protections to help them be successful. Students know that we care about them and will respond with Grace and Accountability every time.
>
> Mrs. Karen Prickett,
> Center Elementary Principal
> Center School District, Kansas City, MO

"Our Kids" Community means that we believe and act in a way to increase success for every student, every adult, every day. In this chapter we will explore how to increase ownership of *all* students throughout the entire adult community. We will also explore what frequently gets in the way of a united adult community and how to avoid some of the most common pitfalls experienced in schools.

Every adult in the building is responsible for every child's success, not only in the classroom but throughout the entire building. Many schools operate in a nine-month mindset, meaning that teachers are responsible for the success of their own students only. However, ideally all adults are responsible for every student in the building during the school year. In order to accomplish this, adults must work together as one whole community rather than as individuals.

Not only do adults have to view each child's success as part of their responsibility, but they must also view the success of other adults as a part of their responsibility. The level of intentionality that is needed to supervise, teach, and individually support students is a frequent focus in staff collaboration. This same level of intentionality must also exist regarding colleagues to develop a cohesive community. When colleagues feel an obligation to all adults the culture becomes one in which the greatest positive impact can be achieved.

I had the opportunity to work with a school that in previous years had experienced high levels of chaos from students and therefore frequently found their adult community polarized and often blaming each other for student misbehavior. During a summer break they came together as a community and were determined to reclaim their school for teaching and learning. They put in tremendous work not only focusing on common area expectations, but also focusing on how to support students who struggle and how to support the adults who work with those students day in and day out. Fast forward to March of that year. I had the opportunity to be with the school and meet with their grade levels. One thing that is somewhat predictable in March prior to the spring break is that the adults can be a bit "grumpy." However, while meeting with the grade levels that specific day, they were problem solving how to continue to support children and adults. One teacher even stated, "I now love coming to work each day because our adults work so well together."

Creating Cohesiveness in the Community by Avoiding Polarization

Creating an "Our Kids" Community must start with intentional messaging from the leaders. Traditionally, school administrators have been asked to do "whatever is best for students." Even though this is the ultimate goal, and the words sound exactly right, this message can cause polarization among the staff. When administrators state to staff "We are going to do what is best for

"Our Kids" Community

students," the covert message is that teachers are currently *not* doing what is best for kids. If teachers perceive negative messaging, they can become isolated and less collaborative with leadership, even, at times, creating negative cliques with colleagues. This can unintentionally undermine the "Our Kids" Community.

One of the most polarizing events in a school community is student discipline. As stated previously, student behavior can be very emotional for teachers and staff. Often, the students with the most difficult behaviors can divide an entire staff. To avoid this polarization, these three things must be intact:

1. Continued focus on the individual student's missing skill (addressed in Chapter 1).
2. Effective planning for individual students (addressed in Chapter 2).
3. Understanding and supporting true Accountability (addressed in Chapter 1).

True Accountability is the foundation of change. So, if a student struggles and is moved to a Safe Seat, the adult must follow up and process through Accountability before that student rejoins the classroom community. Likewise, when a student is moved to the Buddy Room or Recovery Room, the student must process through accountability with the sending teacher. When a student receives an office referral, Accountability must be facilitated by the sending teacher. This can be difficult to accomplish due to how referrals have traditionally been managed. Frequently administrators will state to staff, "Once you have given me the referral, I make decisions about what happens with that student." This is absolutely true! However, a consequence from an administrator does not include Accountability nor does it fix the problem. (A consequence can, however, set bottom lines in the building and cause hesitation for contagious student behavior.) In order to increase cohesiveness regarding discipline, it will require that the administrator ensures each student who receives a referral reconnects and processes through Accountability with the correct adult. Administrators provide Grace and Accountability to staff so staff can provide Accountability and Grace to students. By administrators supporting teachers through Grace and Accountability, the "Our Kids" Community can thrive (see Figure 4.1).

"Our Kids" Community

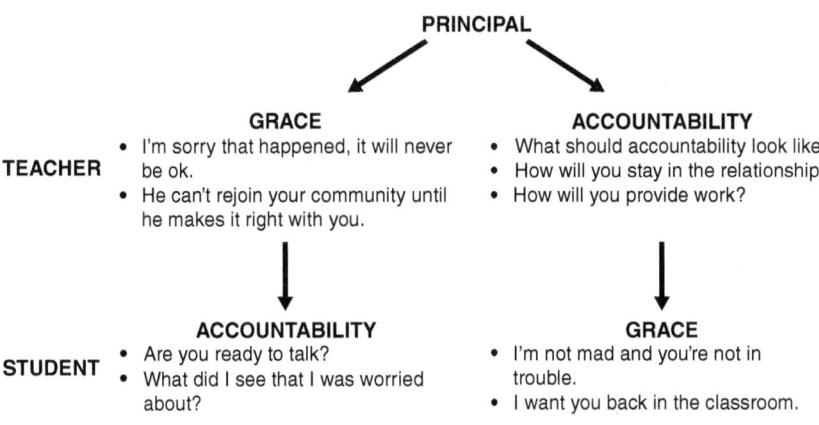

Figure 4.1 Creating a Strong, Impactful Community

Clarifying Management of Behavior

An activity that can assist with the referral process is to create a list of classroom managed vs. office managed behaviors (see Table 4.1). Administrators can also create a list of how they interact with students when they are referred to the office. Many leaders have provided the steps they take with students in the office so that staff are aware of the administrator's role in discipline and the consistency that exists. Even though consequences will rarely feel consistent, the events that occur by the administrator prior to the given consequence are consistent.

Office protocol for referrals (sample):

- Time will be given for the student to de-escalate when needed.
- Discussion about the event will occur.
- Parents will be contacted.
- Consequence will be considered based on:
    - Repetition of the behavior;
    - Publicness of the action;
    - History of the student;
    - Guidance of the school code of conduct.
- Student will return through the BIST continuum when appropriate.
- Student will process with the referring adult.
- Administrator will communicate with teacher prior to student return (when possible).

"Our Kids" Community

Table 4.1 Classroom Managed Behaviors/Office Managed Behaviors

Classroom Managed Behaviors	Office Managed Behaviors
Behaviors that are inappropriate, but minor and can be taken care of by use of the classroom management plan.	Behaviors that are dangerous, potentially illegal, severely disruptive, or significantly violate the rights of others to be addressed by the administration.

• Leaving the classroom without permission
• Minor property damage (e.g. breaking pencils)
• Incomplete homework
• Supplies
• Tattling
• Horseplay
• Non-compliance
• Willful disobedience or defiance
• Minor verbal aggression (e.g. name-calling, inappropriate language/profanity, and tantrums)
• Arguing/verbal conflict
• Work refusal or refusal to participate
• Lying
• Minor stealing
• Cheating
• Gossip, rumors
• Minor unnecessary bodily contact (kicking, hands on, etc.)
• Inappropriate voice control
• Class disruption (noises or minor interruptions, off-task behavior)
	• Leaving school grounds without permission
	• Vandalism
	• Major property damage (breaking iPad)
	• Profanity directed toward adults
	• Safe school violations
	• Substances
	• Fighting (punches, tackling, injury, etc.)
	• Major stealing
	• Harassment (including sexual, racial)
	• Threats
	• Serious property damage
	• Continuous disruptive behaviors (significant loss of instruction—five minutes or more daily—and evidence of prior interventions)
	• Bullying—after district protocol is followed to identify the act as bullying
	   • Repeated
	   • Targeted
	   • Imbalance of power

Intentional Messaging with Colleagues

In Chapter 2 it was stated that colleagues address and support each other. In breaking this down, there are two areas to consider.

First, is it safe to admit that you individually don't know how to help a student who is struggling? In order to make the environment safe to admit the lack of success with a student, colleagues must be intentional about increasing adult vulnerability. Vulnerability around student behavior occurs when the adult with the student concern can share without fear of judgment.

This means that when a teacher states, "I am having so many problems with ...," colleagues respond with empathy and then help identify the student's missing skill. Additionally, colleagues inquire about what the individual teacher might need in order to remain in the relationship with that student.

This type of conversation might sound like this:

Teacher: "I am having so many problems with ...."
Colleague: "I'm sorry that is happening, that has to feel bad. What skill is the student missing? What assistance do you need to be able to support the student?"

Sometimes responses to a teacher stating that they are struggling with an individual student can sound like this: "Really, I don't have any problems with that student." This can be an unintentional, covert message that the other adult is better with students than the colleague who has the concern. Another response could be: "Do you have a relationship with that student?" This response can be perceived as the teacher's fault that the student is struggling due to lack of a relationship.

To create an environment that is safe and vulnerable it is always important to identify and focus on the student's missing skills instead of the lack of adult ability.

Second, is it safe to address colleagues when their actions don't match the building procedures? Educators have the intention of helping students achieve success. However, there are times when adult actions do not match those intentions. In order to make the environment safe to address colleagues, the adult community must establish bottom lines for adult actions during supervision and support of students. Below are areas to consider for increased adult specificity. Just as students in a classroom know their expectations, the adults in the building must also know their responsibilities. The goal in the classroom is to establish a community in which other students help their peers become successful. Likewise, the goal of the adult community is to develop this same concept among the staff members. The following are areas to consider for adult procedures.

Arrival:
1. Who supervises common areas during arrival?
2. Have problem areas been identified (bathrooms, stairwell, lockers)?

3. Are the adults stationed in effective supervisory areas?
4. What time does supervision start and are the adults consistently on time?
5. Are the adults greeting and supervising students?
6. Are the adults taking emotional temperatures?
7. Are the adults using early intervention when procedures aren't followed?
8. Are the adults skilled at confronting students in a direct and respectful manner?
9. What is the exact manner of intervention?
10. Is there a process to identify and plan for students who struggle following the procedures?
11. Is there a plan and backup system to support adults when students don't comply?

Breakfast:
1. What time should adults arrive to supervise breakfast?
2. Do adults have assigned supervision areas in breakfast?
3. Is there a method to document behavior concerns?
4. What is the system for the supervising adult to follow up with the student of concern when needed?

Restrooms:
1. Is there an established plan for supervision of restrooms?
2. Do the adults or students make sure the restroom is clean after each use?
3. Is there an established restroom schedule so that classes do not run into each other on restroom breaks?

Lunch:
1. Are specific adults assigned to specific areas for supervision?
2. Do the adults have a system to document behavior concerns during lunch?
3. How do supervisors communicate with teachers when students struggle in the cafeteria?
4. Is there a system in place for the supervising adults to follow up with students who have a behavior problem?

Hallways:
1. Do elementary teachers walk their students in line?
2. Do teachers walk at about the halfway point of the line?

3. Do teachers have a plan B if students cannot walk in line with the class?
4. Are teachers (secondary) joining any group of students that are three or more?
5. Does everyone verbally intervene in a common way when students misbehave in hallways?

Recess:
1. Is there a level system for recess?
2. How is that communicated to the recess supervisors?
3. Are adults assigned specific areas to supervise at recess?
4. Do adults have a plan if students are not able to manage at recess?

Departure:
1. Do adults have assigned supervision areas during dismissal?
2. Are we holding students who struggle in dismissal accountable the next day?
3. Is there a plan for accountability if problems occur during dismissal?

Once specific expectations are developed, addressing colleagues must be done with kindness and the offer of support when needed. Example: "Are you OK? Do you need anything?"

The Journey of Being an "Our Kids" Community

Teaching in and of itself can be an isolating occupation. In particular, elementary teachers sometimes do not share students with other adults except for specials teachers. Therefore, teachers can feel at times like they are on an island. Working independently to support children often causes levels of frustration and decreases a sense of hope. Therefore, intentionally working toward an "Our Kids" Community, in which teachers can collaborate, support, and celebrate all children, can reinstate a joy in teaching and create an increased sense of belonging.

Becoming an "Our Kids" Community is a journey. To remain in forward progress through this journey there are five observable indicators (schools can use this as a guide for reflection in creating a cohesive community):

1. Teachers work in isolation;
2. Teachers work collaboratively with grade levels or teams;

"Our Kids" Community

3. Teachers support without judgment within their grade levels and teams;
4. Teachers problem solve support of students beyond their grade level/team;
5. The entire educational staff is included in supporting all students.

Think of the five above indicators as you read Table 4.2, which is made up of components that exist in an "Our Kids" Community. Add additional statements as needed. When thinking of each item in Table 4.2, rate your building according to where it is presently (1 = working in isolation, 5 = working as a collaborative, educational staff).

Upon completion of Table 4.2, identify 1–3 initial areas of growth needed in your building and write an action plan. The plan will identify support needed and steps to be taken to assist your team in moving towards a more cohesive "Our Kids" Community.

Table 4.2 Observable Indicators in an "Our Kids" Community

Indicators	Building Ratings
Staff's philosophical foundation of BIST is the why.	
Colleagues provide support for new teachers.	
Staff provide Grace and are willing to develop relationships with any/all students.	
Staff problem-solve students and help them move through the five levels of Accountability.	
Staff follow and enforce the common area expectations with all students.	
Colleagues support and address each other to increase success with common area expectations.	
Classroom management, procedures, and routines are clear and consistent in each classroom.	
Staff track, analyze, and use data to support students who struggle with repetitive behaviors.	
Staff consistently support individual student's needs.	
Behavior plans are developed and implemented to support students with missing skills.	
Individual student plans are consistently communicated and implemented to necessary staff members.	

(Continued)

Table 4.2 (Continued)

Indicators	Building Ratings
Staff help students with missing skills through processing and skill-based coaching.	
Staff consistently communicate with families of individual students who need additional support.	
Staff effectively plan for students as they move through the continuum of change.	
Staff meet monthly to discuss student movement on the continuum of change and revise plans as needed.	

Action Plan Example
Identified area of growth: • Behavior plans are developed and implemented to support students with missing skills. **Plan to address the area:** • Increase all staff capacity to identify, support, and plan for all individual student needs. **Supports needed for growth:** • Vision team will develop ideas of support for students to assist teachers in problem solving. • Revisit tracking system to ensure all teachers are inputting information (reviewed and addressed as needed by administrator). • Building leaders provide training for the vision team regarding planning for individual students. **Steps to take immediately:** • Schedule time for the vision team to meet ASAP. • Determine through grade level discussions the needs regarding training to support students. • Provide staff with ideas of support strategies. **Timeline for growth:** • Vision team receives training to develop skills to support other teachers as they plan for students. • Identify students who need continued or increased support around behavior. • Schedule grade level and vision team meetings monthly to collaborate on students. • Plan follow-up meeting to assess growth.

Action Plan Example
Action Plan #1
Identified area of growth: Big picture plan to address the area: Supports needed for growth: Steps to take immediately: Timeline for growth:
Action Plan #2
Identified area of growth: Big picture plan to address the area: Supports needed for growth: Steps to take immediately: Timeline for growth:
Action Plan #3
Identified area of growth: Big picture plan to address the area: Supports needed for growth: Steps to take immediately: Timeline for growth:

End of Chapter Reflection and Questions

- Review Table 4.1 and update it for your building.
- Complete Table 4.2 and the Action Plan Example.

Increasing Partnerships with Families

I wish I could have been introduced to the BIST philosophy earlier in my career as I feel it would have strengthened my approach to teaching, coaching, and even parenting. Be that as it may, BIST has opened the hearts and minds of our staff to allow us to accept and embrace the fact that behaviors are skills that must be taught in the same manner that we teach academic skills. Our staff now understands the difference between punishment and protection and the limitations that punishment alone has on changing behaviors for life. Our staff has become relentless in their pursuit of holding students accountable through Grace and by meeting students where they are. Our relationships with students, connections with parents, conversations about student behaviors, and our own reactions and responses to students who are out of bounds are significantly improved by the adoption of the BIST philosophy. Our students and families now feel they belong, they matter, and they are worthy rather than just hearing it.

Mr. Todd Jefferson
Ridgeview Elementary Principal
Dunlap, Illinois

Parenting is likely the most vulnerable, emotional journey on which an individual can embark. When that beautiful baby enters the world the journey to support their growth into a productive, caring, giving adult has started. This is by far the most important and scary endeavor one can experience. At approximately age five parents send their children to school where they will spend a significant portion of their life for the next 13 years. Families must be able to trust that schools are striving daily to keep their children safe, allow them to grow, and support them to achieve success. Knowing this, schools have an important obligation to communicate and care for families in a manner that enhances partnerships. Through the family/school partnership, children can blossom into the adults they were meant to be.

Education is the only industry in which every individual has had experience. This can equate to a couple of scenarios for schools to consider. One, since all individuals have experienced education, some parents may feel they are experts and know more than the educational staff. Two, some adults did not have a good experience in school and can be intimidated by the educational system. When intimidated they may either try to avoid it or become defensive quickly when addressed. Knowing these two scenarios forces schools to consider how to intentionally communicate with families in a manner that reduces resistance and encourages collaboration. This squarely puts the onus of partnering with parents on the school's shoulders.

Communicating with Families

The pace of society continues to increase, forcing schools to become more than just educational classrooms. Due to a variety of factors, more and more children are coming to school with social/emotional needs that schools must address. In addressing these increased needs, educators must become more empathetic and intentional, not only when working with students, but also with families. In the following paragraphs we will explore intentional communication that can enhance partnerships with families.

As stated in Larry Brendtro et al.'s (2002) book, *Reclaiming Youth at Risk*, when children struggle in school:

- Schools blame parents first, students second, and themselves third.
- Parents blame schools first, children second, and themselves third.

When this concept comes to life, a polarization can develop that ultimately leaves the child without the required support and therefore lack of success. It is important to remember that families are sending to school the best children they have and that parents want what is best for their child. Thus,

Increasing Partnerships with Families

blaming families for a child's struggle will be counterproductive. What all parents want for their children can be put into four goals:

1. Be as smart as they were made to be;
2. Have friends;
3. Feel good about themselves;
4. Stay out of trouble.

Knowing that all parents ultimately want their children to become productive adults, schools can increase the opportunity for partnerships by initially focusing the conversation on life goals versus classroom concerns. Starting with classroom behavior can often lead to parents becoming defensive and minimizing the issue. Here are examples of intentionally using the above parent goals to start the conversation:

1. Be as smart as they were made to be: "I know you want your son to learn everything he is capable of learning; my fear is that when he is sitting with other students he is frequently talking and not able to focus on the information. It is my job to place him in the best learning location and when it is time to be social, I want him with his friends."
2. Have friends: "I know you want your daughter to have friends. Right now, the way she is interacting with them makes it hard for them to appreciate her. It is my job to supervise her closely to ensure that her conversations with others remain positive."
3. Feel good about themselves: "I know you want your daughter to feel good about herself and when I am constantly correcting her, I don't think this is happening. I'm going to protect her from getting out of bounds by having her walk outside of our line until she is able to remain safe with others."
4. Stay out of trouble: "I know you want your son to be able to stay out of trouble. Right now, on the playground this is hard for him. I am going to have him play in a specific area with a specific friend where he can be safe. As he is better able to manage, I will allow him to play in more areas of the playground."

In the above examples, notice that the parent was never asked to "fix" the school problem by changing things at home. By making a plan that includes

Increasing Partnerships with Families

restrictions or protections at school, it allows the parents to feel less defensive as they are not being blamed or asked to fix the problem. When parents are asked to fix the problem at home, they are often placed in a position of failure. They often commit to the solution at the moment of the conversation as they want to be supportive of the school. However, when it is actually time to change things at home, they often are not able to consistently follow through. Then, when the parents don't follow through, teachers can become frustrated and reduce effort for that child because they see the parent as non-supportive. Schools have frequently defined supportive parents as those that change what happens at home to reinforce what the school is doing. Therefore, making the solution for the student is the parents' responsibility. This thinking can lead to frustration, blame, and polarization thus inhibiting partnerships. If schools begin to define supportive parents as ones who allow the teacher to do what is needed for the child at school, frustration with parents can be reduced.

When parents have a child that is struggling, there is increased emotion. As we know, humans are not made to be emotional and logical at the same time. As shown in the above examples, educators can help reduce the emotion by using language that connects directly to the parent's desire for their child. Educators taking the lead in modeling how to problem solve in a calm productive manner can assist in reducing resistance and therefore allow for the development of support for their child.

As an example: Several years ago, I had the opportunity to work with a family whose 1st grade son was struggling significantly regarding adult directives. The parents willingly came to the school to meet and problem solve. The meeting got off to a bit of a rough start as the 1st grade boy was non-compliant. Initially, dad was trying to get him out from under a table, and when he did come out, he bolted for the door. Mom tried to stop him from leaving the room and consequently caught his fingers in the door which started a significant crying session. Once things calmed down and we were able to visit with his parents, mom turned to me with tears in her eyes and asked, "Is this our fault?" My response was, "The only thing about this whole situation that is your fault is how smart your son is. Everything else is our job to work together so that he can experience success." After hearing this, mom began to relax and we were able to move forward with planning for the child as well as increasing the partnership between school and family.

Communicating Difficult Information

It is critical that parents are aware of a teacher's concern about their child in a very timely manner. This information should never be left to the conversation at parent–teacher conferences.

Communicating by email can often be a temptation as it is quicker and does not require a live time response from the parent. However, it also limits the teacher's ability to express compassion and empathy as there is no tone of voice in an email. Knowing that when a parent hears concerns about their child their emotion will likely increase, it is best to make the first contact regarding a concern either a face-to-face contact or a phone call home. Often when we communicate concerns, parents hear two things that are never actually stated. First, what are you going to do to fix this? Second, they hear, you have the worst kid in school. Again, this information is never stated in those words; however, knowing this is what parents interpret we must deliver concerns in a way that can diffuse emotion and blame.

This can sound like, "I just called to let you know … I don't need you to do anything." "Your child is worthy of success, and it is my job to ensure they experience that here at school." At the time of communication, the teacher should have a plan in mind regarding how they will support the child at school. As stated in Chapter 2, a plan will be based on what a child can't manage and what protections are going to be put in place to ensure they are no longer getting in trouble for these actions. Additionally, teachers should know what skill they are going to teach and practice while the student is restricted.

Here are some additional sentence starters for communication with parents:

- "We've noticed that your child struggles to follow directions. Do you ever worry about that? That is what we see at school, and it is our job to help in that area."
- "It is my job to make sure that your child knows I am on their side."
- "Here are some protections that we want to put in place to support your child so they can experience success more frequently."
- "I can hear you are worried that I'm not being fair. That is a great reason to be concerned. Do you have a minute to talk through how I can better support your child?"

- "What do you think would be helpful for …?"
- "I know this is hard."
- "We can work together."

Parent–Teacher Conferences

When parents attend conferences (on site or virtually) educators must remember that, although school is a second home for staff, to many parents it is not a place of comfort and can even be intimidating and create anxiety. Knowing this, it is essential that conferences are set up as a family friendly event that include positive information about each child. To increase the welcoming atmosphere, many schools provide drinks and snacks as a part of the conference process. Childcare for younger children can also be considered so that families can be completely focused on the conversation. Additionally, ensure that directions to classrooms are clearly marked. Also, making the conference environment comfortable by providing adult-size chairs, sitting on the same side of the table, and providing visual examples of excellent work can make great strides in decreasing discomfort and increasing collaboration.

When conferencing with parents, teachers should practice good communication skills such as:

- Be calm and composed;
- Eliminate judgment and evaluation;
- Be concrete and concise;
- Be honest and direct without being emotional;
- Accept the parents' reaction;
- Don't be defensive;
- Invite the parents to ask questions.

Parent conferences only occur a couple of times per year. This is not the place to do in-depth planning for children, but rather the opportunity to show children's work and progress. If there is a concern that will take additional time to address, be sure to schedule follow-up time with the parents.

Increasing Partnerships with Families

Conferencing with Frustrated/Angry Parents

There are times when parents contact teachers because they feel frustrated. This frustration is often driven by something their child has shared with them. Typically, when a child shares information with a parent, there may be some gaps in the actual events. It can be a natural tendency to defend school actions if it sounds as though the parent has not received accurate information. If staff members defend their actions, the chances of escalating the frustration increase. When parents are frustrated with the school or the individual teacher it can sometimes help to start with an apology. This means employing the concept of being effective over being right.

After the opening apology, it can help to thank the parent for the feedback and validate how they might feel. This can assist in diminishing frustration and increase the opportunity for problem solving. Remember that anger is never a primary emotion, and when parents are frustrated it is typically driven by fear that:

1. The school is being unfair;
2. The child is having a similar, negative experience such as the parent had;
3. The parent feels inadequate;
4. The child is not OK, and the parent is scared.

If educators can take a deep breath and get beneath these emotions, the parent may experience relief that their fears were recognized. At that point the conversation can often move into one of sharing accurate information and problem solving.

A conversation might sound like this:

> "I am so sorry I didn't do a better job communicating. I can hear that you are worried that I might be unfair. If you have a minute, I would like to share the goal I have for your child. I want your child to feel good about themselves and when I am constantly calling out their name for talking this can't feel good. My plan is to sit him away from other students during direct instruction time. When it is time to be social, I certainly want him with his friends. What concerns do you have

with this plan? Would you like me to follow up in a week? Would you like the follow up to be in email, text, phone call, or face to face?"

If the parent is not able to calm down or continues to escalate, the conversation should likely be stopped and scheduled for a different time.

Positive Communication

Every parent wants to hear that their child is the teacher's favorite student. Each educator has approximately 18–28 favorite students in each classroom. By communicating something personal that has been noticed about the child, it helps parents trust that the teacher is personally invested in the child's success. Of course, everyone knows that positive deposits in the bank make it easier to make a withdrawal when necessary. When communicating with families of a struggling student, rules of thumb are:

- Communicate often;
- Communicate positives;
- Communicate goals;
- Communicate progress;
- Communicate care for the family.

Information Specific for Parents

When utilizing the BIST Continuum (Chapter 2) in the school system, parents should have information up front about the *why* and the *how* of supporting students. Frequently schools have addressed the information in their Back to School Nights. They also have informational brochures available for parents. Lastly, many teachers will include BIST Bytes in their parent newsletters. A parent pamphlet can be accessed at bist.org.

Supporting Parents within Their Homes

Many parents are struggling with the day to day raising of children. Once a partnership is established with the school it is common for parents to support their child differently at home. Some quick tips for this are:

- Establishing boundaries;
- Creating procedures and routines;
- Pre-coaching children on missing skills;
- Problem solving to learn and grow;
- Family meetings.

For additional information go to bist.org – Parenting to Create Positive Results.

End of Chapter Reflection and Questions

- **How are you communicating your care for students with all families?**
- **Identify families to make a stronger connection, and discover what initial actions are needed for this partnership.**
- **What support do staff members need when communicating with families that might resist the information?**

Reference

Brendtro, Larry K., Brokenleg, Martin and Van Bockern, Steve, 2002. *Reclaiming youth at risk; Our hope for the future.* Bloomington, IN: Solution Tree.

Enhancing Our Vision, Growing Our Impact

There is a blessing in everything and one of the biggest blessings I have encountered as a building leader has been my work with the philosophy of BIST. I have witnessed the positive impact that BIST has had on the students I serve and the teachers I work alongside every day. The key word that transcends when implementing BIST with fidelity is relationships. The relationships that are fostered through this work are due to the collaboration and reflection of staff members. These relationships are necessary on an ongoing basis for true change to occur with children. The ownership students feel when they achieve their behavioral goals is inspirational and increases motivation for continued success. The vision team can support teachers through this process of student change. Achievements inspire staff to continue to collaborate in a way that allows for behavioral transformation of students. The philosophy of BIST is simple. 'It is NEVER OK to be hurtful, and it is NEVER OK to be disruptive." All inappropriate choices fall into one of these two categories; therefore, staff can quickly identify the work that needs to be done with the student. Schools must continue to make behavior and social skills as important as academic skills if we are going to create a safer, more productive society. BIST helps schools accomplish this goal. It has changed me forever as a leader. It allows me to coach staff on how to foster significant relationships through both Grace and Accountability.

Mrs. Jennie Alderman
Franklin Smith Elementary School Principal
Blue Springs, MO

Developing a vision is the most critical part of school leadership. A vision is the road map for the entire staff. It takes time and experience to develop this. In the next section we will focus on how to enhance school culture beyond academic issues to include the emotional and behavioral success of children. This includes how adults will interact with children and support each other.

Why Do You Need a Vision for the Culture Regarding Behavior?

If there is not a specific vision for the culture regarding student behavior, then every individual brings their own belief in how to support and interact with students. This can result in splintered, unpredictable support. When interactions are inconsistent, the opportunity for student success may be limited. Table 6.1 can guide in identifying concerns within the school culture and the positive results when cohesiveness is established.

Table 6.1 Indicators or Concerns

Indicators or Concerns	How Staff Benefit from Change	How Students Benefit from Change
Staff isolation	Increased collegiality	Increased adult support
Continued staff frustration	Calmer presence	Calmer classroom atmosphere
Lack of engagement	Increased teacher ownership	Increased engagement in the learning process
Polarization	Cohesive mindset	Consistency in support
Consistent misbehavior in classrooms	Confidence to address behaviors	Decreased classroom disruption
Teacher turnover	Consistency among staff	Predictability throughout the building
Inconsistent development of relationships	Balance of Grace and Accountability	Higher level of success behaviorally and emotionally

What Is Your Vision for Student Behavior and the Culture That Cultivates It?

Student behavior and social emotional learning must be major components in the vision. This will ultimately determine how staff interact with students in general, how they interact with students who struggle with behavior, and how they interact with each other, both in the building and in the parking lot. To develop or enhance this vision the following are some questions for reflection and growth.

What Do You Believe about Staff's Responsibility Regarding Student Behavior?

Leaders know exactly what they desire for children academically based on state and district standards. However, behavioral issues are frequently addressed through handbooks and guiding discipline policies. When these are the commonly used practices that dictate adult response to behavior, there is minimal room to look at students and support them based on their individual needs.

In contrast, leaders that truly have a vision for students who struggle, believe that staff have an obligation to ensure that all children experience success behaviorally. Therefore, staff must have permission to differentiate behavioral support that is similar to academic support. To achieve this, leaders must be able to articulate what is involved in success for every child and the adult's responsibility for that success. Behaviorally, each child should be able to:

1. Have an overwhelming feeling and make good choices;
2. Be okay when others are not okay;
3. Do things when they don't want to or when it is hard.

Here is an example of a school vision with some critical components:

1. The balance of Grace and Accountability;
2. The concept of teaching and protecting;
3. Students who struggle are missing skills;
4. Shared ownership when students struggle;
5. Every child, every adult, every day.

A sample vision:

> "As we approach a new school year, I want to be clear about what I believe our vision is when it comes to providing consistency of care for all children. The foundation of our thinking must be based on Grace and Accountability. Grace is the relationship that is unconditional for every child, even though children may try to reject us. Accountability is the ability and willingness to problem solve with children when they make a mistake. This helps them increase: their critical thinking skills, their resilience, and their ability to overcome mistakes, and therefore increases their confidence and effort. How we achieve this is through the concept of teaching and protecting vs. punishment and forgiveness. That doesn't mean we will never have consequences for children in this building. It means that when children are missing a skill, we will always look at how to protect them from what they can't manage and teach them the skill that will allow them to achieve success more frequently. We must also commit to the thinking that when children struggle repetitively in behavior it is about a missing skill not an adult inadequacy. In order to assist all children in higher levels of behavioral success within our building, we have shared ownership: "Every Child, Every Adult, Every Day" so that children experience success daily."

By delivering this type of message to the entire staff, the groundwork is being laid for the mindset transformation regarding kids who struggle. The bottom line has also been stated that punishment will not be the mode of support when children are missing skills behaviorally.

When Children Struggle What Must Occur to Achieve Long-Term, Lasting Change Beyond the Classroom?

Accountability through relationships is the key to long-term, sustainable change. Change is a lengthy and arduous journey with multiple obstacles to overcome. For adults to provide ongoing Accountability to children they must have consistent, like-minded collaboration. This collaboration includes not only how to support children, but also support for the adults working with them.

What Role Must Staff Members Have in the Behavioral Success of Children?

All staff members are responsible for student achievement academically and behaviorally. When obstacles arise, teachers must have the confidence and competence to create supports that will allow students to experience success more frequently. Additionally, staff must have the ability to teach students new life skills so that they can manage any environment appropriately. This can only occur when staff feel a level of ownership and obligation for all students. As individual students are identified, building leaders support adults as they help children in the journey to success.

What Is the Required Knowledge that Staff Must Have to Live the Vision Daily?

The most critical component of the vision is a consistent mindset of the staff that all kids can achieve success through Grace and Accountability. Staff members must have a belief that children who are missing skills will not change through punishment.

What Resources Do You Need to Fulfill the Vision?

As a leader begins to implement their vision around a specific foundation, there should be training. This training can be formal or informal. There should be a shared message prior to the training in order to establish what learning is desired and required, as well as what the ultimate outcomes can be. If the vision requires specific actions that do not previously exist, the training should be formalized. The power of outside coaches facilitating the training is that they have the opportunity to remain detached from the emotion elicited by change. It will be important that the training aligns with what the leader envisions the culture should become. If previous school practices are going to change based on the training, there will need to be time built in for leadership teams to reflect and create processes for those changes. In delivering the required changes, it will be necessary to include the why to increase staff buy in.

After the initial processes have been taught and the implementation begins it will be beneficial for a school to receive assistance from an outside coach. As Marzano et al. (2005) state: "To ensure a non-evaluative culture, the coach should not have management responsibilities over the coachee. The non-evaluative coach fosters receptivity and tolerance." The process of coaching starts with learning and progresses through development of skills, application of new actions and thinking, and eventually innovation in which true ownership occurs. In the process of implementation, there must be time built into staff schedules that allow for conversations on what is going well and what is not going well. These conversations should be non-judgmental to allow for mistakes in the growth phase. Additionally, staff will need time for practice of new words and actions in order to ensure internalization of the new habits. Lastly, there will need to be a system to ensure that growth of both staff and students is taking place.

When developing a vision about students who struggle, it will be important to know the expectations that they should achieve behaviorally. Teachers know academically what is expected of students each year. This should be equally true for behavior. A vision for student behavior must have a pervasive, philosophical foundation. It is necessary to be explicit regarding the thinking about children that includes *both* Grace and Accountability.

How Do You Share Your Vision?

When sharing a vision, it is important to share frequently both in small groups and whole staff settings. There are a number of methods in which to share the vision. These methods can be both verbal and written information. Here is a list of ways in which to share the vision:

1. Staff meetings;
2. Department or grade level meetings;
3. Individual teacher meetings;
4. Weekly bulletins;
5. Posters in school (hallways, teacher workroom, office);
6. Parent newsletters.

How Do You Concisely Articulate Information in a Manner that Provides Clarity?

It will be important for leaders to deliver their vision to the entire staff at one time in order for each staff member to hear a consistent message. However, a one-time delivery of information does not allow for individuals to assimilate the information into true meaning or connect the information to actions. Thus, assisting staff in acquiring the leader's vision will require the repetition of the message and consistency in the language used.

The work of providing structured time for conversations and increased understanding of the components in the vision begins. These conversations will help translate thinking into actions.

How Do Teams Utilize Structured Time to Increase Clarity?

Grade level, multi-disciplinary teams, or content team meetings, are the most ideal time frames to allow for safe, structured conversations. To ensure that these conversations are productive and do not become problem admiring or storytelling, it may be helpful to provide a meeting protocol and a list of questions. It is important for the leader or teacher leaders to be active participants in these conversations. Here is an example of some questions that can provide structure to ensure clarity and buy-in of the vision:

1. What are your positive takeaways regarding our vision?
2. What doubts or reservations do you have?
3. What questions are there regarding Grace and Accountability?
4. Are you able to identify which skill a struggling student is missing?

Additionally, during weekly grade level/team meetings there will need to be time to discuss practical actions and ensure those actions match the vision of creating a higher level of success for all children.

Practical actions to be discussed:

1. Early intervention to redirect behavior;
2. Common language of intervention;
3. Processing to guide accountability for individual students;
4. Planning for individual students to increase success;

5. Outlasting continuum of change;
6. Data collection regarding student concerns.

How Do You Support Individual Teacher Conversations?

Providing time for conversations with individual staff members will allow the leader the opportunity to answer individual questions, close gaps in understanding, as well as identify concerns that do not align with the vision. When supporting individual staff members, it will be important for the leader to additionally provide time to model the desired actions with students. This is a powerful method to increase buy-in, model appropriate actions, and increase credibility.

How Do You Inspire and Motivate People to Participate in Your Vision?

To get others to buy into a vision requires inspiration and motivation. Inspiration is created by stimulating individuals to feel something or do something with a bigger purpose. Going beyond individual empowerment to instill staff efficacy is critical. To create staff efficacy, a leader must assist staff members to see how their actions create success for children beyond the classroom. An example is: Having a student that struggled and ultimately experienced success return to talk to the staff. Here is a quote from a 7th grade student who returned to talk to the staff at his elementary school on a professional development day. "You all are my heroes, that is why I am OK."

Motivation is the process that initiates, guides, and maintains behavior. Once staff are inspired with a vision that has a bigger purpose, motivation will play a role in the continued enactment of the vision. One of the most motivating factors is success itself. The identification and celebration of their successes must be a continual process.

Strategies to increase motivation for staff are:

- *Set goals to be attained.* In setting goals for staff, there must be collaboration to determine priorities in the journey. Additionally, making the goals public for staff allows individuals to assess personally the role they are

playing in meeting the goals. It will be important to have a time frame in which the goals are reviewed and, of course, there will be a need to revise as growth occurs.
- *Create safety for failure.* The course of any journey will provide equal opportunity for both success and "failure." It will be critical to allow staff members to reflect and vocalize their perceived failures in order to create safety and learning. As a leader it will be important to state your expectations regarding mistakes and how to learn from them in a non-judgmental environment. Also, it will be important to model when you personally have made a mistake and what you have learned in the process.
- *Celebrate staff successes.* Peers supporting each other in their successes can minimize competition for recognition. Creating a culture in which colleagues celebrate success with each other will increase motivation and momentum.
- *Provide opportunity for student voices to be heard.* Learning from the success of children will additionally create motivation. Allowing students to articulate their success will not only help them grow, but also encourage staff to continue their journey of support.

How Do You Hold Teachers Accountable to Your Vision?

As with any initiative, it is critical to allow time for learning and practicing. Once staff have been given time to grow their skill set, it is necessary to establish bottom lines for actions that ensure the vision comes to fruition. Table 6.2 is a rubric providing BIST components that can be utilized to establish bottom lines for staff.

Table 6.2 Rubric for Adult Accountability

Definitions	Least Effective				Most Effective
	1	2	3	4	5
	Grace				
Give students what they need, not what they deserve—whether they want or don't want the support.	Adult removes the student without giving Grace	Adult uses combination of Grace and punishment	Adult uses Grace without Accountability in an attempt to maintain the relationship	Adult uses Grace with inconsistent standards of Accountability	Adult uses Grace with high standards of Accountability
Stay in the relationship when students reject you.	Adult severs the relationship	Adult attempts inconsistent relationship building		Adult maintains the relationship	Adult is consistent in maintaining the relationship
Maintain high standards while supporting students.				OR Adult inconsistent in maintaining relationship	

(Continued)

Table 6.2 (Continued)

Definitions	Least Effective				Most Effective
	1	2	3	4	5
Accountability					
I did it—ownership with honesty.	Adult not holding student accountable	Adult holds student accountable for actions	Adult holds student accountable for actions, apology, and "It's a problem," but no partnership	Adult holds student accountable for actions, apology, problem, and consequences with or without partnership	Adult holds student accountable for actions, apology, problem, consequences, and coachability with partnership
I'm sorry.		Adult holds student accountable for an apology			
It's a problem in my life partnership.					
I accept consequences					
I accept and need help—coachability.					
Teaching					
Teach life skills to change a student's ability to manage: I can …. (a) be angry or overwhelmed and not get in trouble; (b) be okay even if others are not okay; (c) do something even if I don't want to or it is difficult.	Adult does not teach life skills	Adult inconsistently teaches life skills	Adult teaches life skills and begins to coach life skills	Adult coaches life skills	Adult consistently coaches life skills to make changes in student behaviors

	Protecting			
Restriction based on what the student's repetitious behaviors show (s)he can't manage.	Adult gives student no restrictions	Adult gives student punishment based restrictions	Adult gives student restrictions not based on repetitious behavior	Adult gives student restrictions based on repetitious behavior but no adult follow-through	Adult gives student restrictions matching repetitious behavior and consistently follows through
	Early Intervention			
Stop the behavior when you see it, not when you feel it.	Adult does not intervene to stop behaviors	Adult gives numerous redirects without stopping or identifying behaviors	Adult identifies and addresses behaviors with numerous redirects	Adult immediately addresses behaviors when observed with more than one redirect	Adult immediately addresses behaviors when observed with no more than one redirect
Give one verbal redirect per activity.					

(Continued)

Table 6.2 (Continued)

Definitions		Least Effective			Most Effective
	1	2	3	4	5
Caring Confrontation					
"I see…."	Adult yells or uses unkind language/voice tone to address the problem	Adult ignores the problem	Adult uses inconsistent confrontation	Adult confronts consistently and uses inconsistent language/voice tone	Adult confronts consistently
"Can you…."			Adult uses inconsistent language/voice tone	OR	Adult uses language that increases partnership and reduces resistance from student
"Even though…."				Adult uses consistent language/voice tone and confronts inconsistently	
Adults speak through intentions, not emotions and use intentional language to reduce resistance.					

	Processing				
Re-establish the relationship. Problem solve to hold the student accountable.	Adult allows student back in class without processing	Adult uses inconsistent processing with no teacher/student Accountability	Adult uses consistent processing with inconsistent teacher/student accountability	Adult uses consistent processing with consistent accountability but no re-establishment of relationship	Adult problem-solves with student through accountability and re-establishes the relationship
Protective Planning					
Create supports, restriction, and practice for students "in trouble" and who don't stop getting "in trouble."	Adult has no student plan in place	Adult has student plan in place with no missing skills identified and no student check-in or follow-up	Adult has student plan in place which matches missing skills but not follow-up or check-in	Adult has student plan in place which matches missing skills with follow-up or check-in	Adult has student plan in place which matches missing skills with follow-up or check-in
				Adult does not have team review or make parent contact	Adult has team review and makes parent contact

(Continued)

Table 6.2 (Continued)

Definitions		Least Effective				Most Effective
		1	2	3	4	5
Practice						
Create rote muscle memory. Do it right, more than you have done it wrong.		Adult has student plan in place but no practice of missing skills is included	Adult has student plan in place with practice but the practice does not match the missing skill	Adult has student plan in place which matches the missing skill but practice is inconsistent	Adult has student plan in place which matches the missing skill but no ongoing practice	Adult has student plan in place which includes daily practice of missing skill on an ongoing basis
Outlasting Continuum						
Non-compliance, compliance, partnership, independence.		Adult has no discussion of behavior with student	Adult gets student to apologize and understand why it is wrong	Adult maintains restrictions until student is compliant	Adult maintains restrictions until student owns the problem	Adult stays in relationship with student
		Adult allows student to go to class without consequences.	Adult puts no restrictions in place	Adult checks with student 2–3 times per week	Adult checks with student 2–3 times per week	Adult maintains restrictions until partnership is reached
		Adult does no relationship building.	Adult does not build relationship			

	Balanced Discipline				
Have the ability to stay balanced (not enabling, not counter-aggressive) when working with students who struggle.	Adult does not problem solve for student	Adult problem solves for student	Adult enables student behaviors with multiple redirects before problem solving begins	Adult inconsistently problem solves with student	Adult consistently problem solves with student to identify missing skill
	Adult emotions visible	Adult emotions visible	Adult has emotions under control	Adult has emotions under control	Adult has emotions under control
	Skill-Based Coaching				
Relationship based conversation.	Adult does not identify missing skill	Adult identifies missing skill but there is no coaching or practice	Adult identifies missing skill with one time coaching or practice	Adult identifies missing skill with inconsistent coaching or practice	Adult identifies missing skill with consistent coaching or practice
Coaching students on their skill deficits.	Adult ignores the student behavior	Adult does not establish a relationship with student	Adult attempts to establish a relationship with student but not ongoing	Adult attempts to establish a relationship with student but does not maintain it	Adult establishes and maintains a relationship with student even if student does not want it
	Adult does not establish a relationship with student				

(Continued)

Table 6.2 (Continued)

Definitions	Least Effective				Most Effective
	1	2	3	4	5
Recovery Process					
Uses restricting, teaching and coaching to the point of life change. Movement through the outlasting continuum.	Adult does not maintain restrictions when student reaches compliance	Adult has restrictions in place when student reaches compliance, but no teaching or coaching takes place	Adult has restrictions in place when student reaches compliance with teaching or coaching on an as-needed basis	Adult has restrictions in place when student reaches compliance with inconsistent teaching or coaching	Adult has restrictions in place when student reaches compliance with consistent teaching or coaching to the point of ownership and partnership
Partnership					
Includes honesty, problem-solving, and common goals	Adult lectures students with little or no problem-solving nor goal setting	Adult begins with processing but ends with lecturing and no problem-solving nor goal setting	Adult processes and problem-solves with student but is inconsistent in goal setting and practicing life skills	Adult processes, problem-solves, sets goals, and practices life skills with student in caring, non-confrontational manner	Adult and student have common goals

Felt; not quantified.	Adult severs relationship with student	Adult does not maintain relationship with student	Adult maintains an inconsistent relationship with student	Adult works to maintain relationship with student	Adult assists student in practicing life skills to rote muscle memory level.
					Adult and student recognize student will be successful without adult

Rubric for Adult Accountability

With Table 6.2 the leader has been able to provide a description of what is ideal in each of the focus areas. Each individual will progress at their own rate, and some may need individualized support.

Being an administrator means not only sharing your vision, but also being willing to have the difficult conversations to hold staff accountable to your vision. Leaders can always be busy enough to postpone the hard, sometimes uncomfortable, conversations. However, those difficult conversations and a leader's ability and willingness to have them is a significant part of creating a high functioning team. As Brene Brown (2018) says, "Clear is kind, unclear is unkind."

A mistake frequently made is announcing to the whole staff a concern that only involves a few individuals. An example is: one or two staff members wear jeans when not appropriate and the announcement to the staff is "Don't wear jeans until designated days." This can damage staff morale and make the individuals that are doing the right thing feel defeated. Address individual concerns privately and in a timely manner. Caring confrontation is meant for adults as well as students.

Developing a safe, open, and honest environment in which to problem solve is very helpful for the coaching session. Some questions to consider in preparation for the meeting are:

- How can I understand the perspective and feeling from the individual's point of view?
- How can I ensure I take into account the individual's well-being?
- How can I use problem solving to help the individual be more productive and successful?

The following are some sentence starters to use in coaching adults toward change.

Empathizing and validating:
- *I know this is hard ...*
- *I have also felt ...*
- *I have struggled ...*
- *It must feel awful ...*

Getting to the point:
- *I noticed you were upset.*
- *I noticed you were angry.*
- *I noticed that this has been hard for you.*
- *I noticed that this is not working for you.*

Encouraging and addressing ownership of the problem:
- *Do you worry that …?*
- *Why do you think …is happening?*
- *What concerns do you have in relation to …?*

Defining intentions and expectations:
- *It is my job to help you with this problem …*
- *You don't have to do this alone …*
- *This situation can be made better.*
- *It is important that things feel better for you …*
- *I want this situation to be more productive for you …*
- *I think you will feel more successful if you …*
- *I don't think you will feel relief until we get …*

Getting feedback:
- *What do you think of these ideas?*
- *What do you like or dislike about this approach?*
- *How can we get this done?*
- *What will keep us from accomplishing this?*
- *How can I make sure the standards are upheld?*

Explaining a follow-up plan:
- *I will check back every week …*
- *I will need to …*
- *Could you please have … by …?*
- *I will know if we need to make changes by …*

A vision is more than just words publicly posted. It is a living, evolving way of life. A vision that endures, must not rely on only one individual. Sustainability requires staff capacity, competence, and confidence.

End of Chapter Reflection and Questions

- Modify or enhance a vision for how you will handle students who struggle in your building/classroom.
- Brainstorm ways in which to share your vision with your building/classroom?
- As a team (grade level/building) fill out the provided rubric on establishing bottom lines for staff.

References

Marzano, Robert J., Walters, Timothy and McNulty, Brian A., 2005. *School leadership that works: From research to results.* Alexandria, VA: ASCD.

Brown, Brené, 2018. *Dare to lead: Brave work. Tough conversations. Whole hearts.* New York, NY: Random House.

Capacity: Increasing Ownership

When I first began teaching, my understanding of BIST was exclusively centered around the logistical components of the BIST Model. As a first-year teacher, I didn't know what I didn't know on many fronts, and BIST was no exception to that! Because I (incorrectly) saw BIST as simply a logistical model, I failed to grasp the transforming effects BIST can generate and spent an entire year having little to no impact with the students who needed me the most. It wasn't until I attended my first BIST training the summer after my first year of teaching that I truly understood what BIST was—a philosophy that should guide every decision we make for and about students. Listening to and learning from Marty that week changed not only my sense of obligation to students who struggle, it truly changed my life. From that point on, I began to see my purpose as not only teaching students content, but working to have a life impact with those students who deserved it the least but needed it the most. Today, it is truly an honor to be a part of the BIST team and support teachers and schools in all the incredible work they do for students and their success.

Mr. Nick Oddo
Former Middle School Teacher
BIST Manager/Consultant
Kansas City, MO

"I was working as hard as I could work, and the staff felt like I was not available or supportive. That's when I knew that I can't be the only person putting this vision in place." This statement is from a building leader who now utilizes teacher leadership very differently. Ultimately, the success of administrators in supporting students who struggle comes from creating competence within their staff. Creating teacher capacity will ensure great results. The kind of results that cause teachers to want to work in the building, and the kind of results that make the culture one that other schools want to emulate. True change at the practical level is completed through teachers who support the vision of the leader. The vision serves as the belief system for the building. As Simon Sinek (2009) says, "progress is fueled by the undying belief that the future is bright." This hope helps to build the capacity.

Creating Capacity to Ensure the Vision

Building teacher capacity starts with a leader's intentional message about how to effectively support children who struggle. It also requires selecting teacher leaders who have a cohesive mindset regarding teaching and protecting children. This identified group of teachers is the beginning of developing capacity among staff. When developing capacity there are three areas to consider:

1. Mindset (foundational thinking);
2. Skill competence (practical strategies);
3. Vision team leadership.

Mindset

Creating a cohesive mindset will require ongoing discussion in order for teachers to solidify their thinking. This has two results: (1) Teachers increase their consistency in thinking and (2) it begins to influence the culture in their classrooms.

Here is a list of actions that will increase consistency in foundational thinking:

- Training in philosophical foundations;
- Site visits to schools more advanced in their journey;
- Team members sharing with staff/colleagues;
- Space to discuss concerns and next steps.

As foundational thinking becomes more ingrained, it will also require the development of skills. When examining existing policies and procedures administrators and teacher leaders will need to spend time determining if the procedures need to be changed or if the thinking behind the actions need to be changed. Often the action of the skill is correct but the why behind the actions will need to be examined and adjusted. An example that could have the right actions and not the correct thinking might be a movement to the Safe Seat. This is a practice that has been in existence for years but the thinking behind this action is often "time out" and "you're in trouble." The shift in thinking becomes: "You're not in trouble but it is my job (teacher) to put you in a place where you can do the right thing and experience success."

The mindset must be one of growth and willingness to try new ideas. Additionally, it must include the belief that failure is temporary and there is an opportunity for learning and growth.

Skill Competence

As mindsets begin to shift, skill competence must be addressed. To increase mastery, teachers will need initial training about the numerous skills that will be employed (as outlined in Chapter 2). An example of skill enhancement is teaching the exact words to be used in specific situations. Instead of "How many times do I have to tell you?" the shift in words can be to "I don't want you to be in trouble, can you let me help you?" Teaching the exact words to say will increase success with students.

Skills that will need to be taught are:

1. How quickly behavior is addressed and redirected;
2. How adults redirect students both verbally and non-verbally;
3. The intentionality with which adults supervise children;
4. How adults problem solve with students to increase Accountability;
5. How supports are put in place for individual students so they do not just stop behavior but create long-term change;
6. Prevention based coaching to increase student mastery.

As the skills are implemented, opportunity for practice must be provided as well as time to reflect on both success and failures.

As Brené Brown (2012) says, "learning is a vulnerable process." This is true not only for students, but also for staff. When opportunity for reflection occurs, vulnerability can be increased by providing concise talking points, modeling by administration, and celebration of success. Here are some example questions to be used during adult reflection time:

1. What skill have you focused on? (Examples: early intervention, intentional language to reduce resistance.)
2. Have you used this skill? If not, why not?
3. What went well?
4. What didn't go well?
5. How did you feel?
6. What will you do differently next time?

Teachers should know in advance the questions that will be asked of them during reflection conversations. Additionally, the conversations must be formatted in a manner that is judgment free and allows for failure and ultimately growth.

As schools more closely examine their current practices it is likely that some of the actions will need to be changed. An example of this might be walking laps at recess. This strategy rarely creates long-term change and therefore may need to be altered to support the individual student in what they can't manage.

Vision Team Leadership

When administrators establish a team to lead their vision, it is predicated on teacher-leader credibility. There are two areas that establish credibility:

1. The leader's perception of the individual;
2. The staff's perception of the individual.

A strong leader identifies teachers that bring strengths the principal does not possess. This allows for diversity of thinking and skills to make the team stronger. Additionally, administrators must trust that the teacher leaders can be coached in a direct manner. Teacher leaders must be able to follow through on suggestions and course corrections during implementation.

Lastly but perhaps most importantly is the perception held by other staff members. Staff must trust the selected leaders, or they will not follow them. Establishing trust with teachers requires the ability to be empathetic, to have integrity in difficult situations, and the ability to collaborate with colleagues in a non-judgmental, supportive manner.

The vision team can be a factor in helping buildings move from a "my kids, your kids" to an "Our Kids" Community. This team holds responsibilities on different levels. They are the drive behind the philosophical foundation and the energy to stay strong while working with difficult students. Additionally, they support staff in planning individually for increased student success.

When a building implements any new concept, there will be energy and excitement for new successes. However, there will also be challenges when staff members feel they have not been successful. Vision team members should plan for these challenges and the emotions brought forth in order to create an environment in which growth can occur from the obstacles. (Refer to Appendix 7.1).

Creating the Tipping Point

Malcolm Gladwell (2000) describes the "tipping point" phenomenon as that magic moment when an idea, trend, or social behavior crosses a threshold, tips, and spreads like wildfire. Just as a single sick person can start an epidemic of the flu, so too can a small but precisely targeted push cause a fashion trend, the popularity of a new product, or a drop in the crime rate. (Refer to Appendix 7.2).

As capacity grows it is helpful to be strategic in how to support the rest of the staff. Appendix 7.2 assesses areas of strengths and obstacles throughout the building regarding content knowledge and adult actions. Appendix 7.3 is for leadership to focus on the individual skills of staff and what support they need to increase momentum toward a more cohesive community. Frequently at the beginning of an initiative, leaders will focus on the staff who may appear resistant. To build capacity toward the tipping point, the administrator must help the team support the staff that are in partnership and compliance. This is how change will occur more quickly. Here are the adult definitions of the four areas in the Adult Continuum of Change (refer to Appendix 7.3):

- **Independence**—this tends to be a small percentage of the staff. These are the teachers that are innovators and will put energy into implementation. This type of teacher can embrace change and can assimilate changes quickly.

Likely, these teachers will serve on the vision team initially. They can mentor staff and lead problem solving in the initial phases of an initiative.
- **Partnership**—these are the staff members that are game changers for a building due to their ability to be empathetic as other colleagues try new methods. Because this type of teacher can have a critical, positive impact on colleagues, it will be important that several of these teachers are part of the vision team. They are at the forefront of change but tend to be more methodical in their approach of implementation.
- **Compliance**—these staff members could be slower to try new strategies, typically for two reasons: (1) What they have been doing feels effective and (2) they want to wait and see if what others are doing actually works. Sometimes these teachers do the work simply because a leader said it should be done.
- **Non-Compliance**—this is typically a very small percentage of the staff. Often, these are the staff members that have experienced numerous building initiatives that they perceive have not been successful. They typically believe if they wait long enough things will go back to the way they were, and life will continue without further disruptions. These teachers tend to have a fixed mindset about student behavior.

Sustainability

What causes actions to be sustainable within a school building? Many schools will start new initiatives which are helpful to students; however, within months the actions of the adults begin to subside and the impact for students is diminished. Initially, when an initiative is implemented, there is energy and excitement about the possibilities. However, as Dr. Patrick Dolan (1994) says in *Restructuring Our Schools*, "the system-in-place will actively resist change. The system works hard at maintaining its equilibrium or its 'Steady State.' It will resist change in fundamental and powerful ways." Thus, any changes made in schools could be challenging. Without the "why" driving the daily actions, the "how" will lose its impact. Therefore, leadership must incorporate a method to revisit the "why" on a consistent basis.

I have had the awesome opportunity to work with a vision team in an elementary school for the past seven years. They have grown from a team that is trying to understand and live the philosophy of the BIST Model to now consistently and frequently working as an "Our Kids" Community. If a teacher is struggling with a student, they can contact their vision team representative and ask for assistance. The available members of the team will then meet that evening after school to talk about what support the student needs as well as what support the teacher needs in order to remain in the relationship with the student. Often the administrators are not involved directly in these planning meetings but are simply notified of the outcome. This is a great example of sustainable capacity at the teacher level. Additionally, through these timely and effective actions, all teachers in the building feel supported.

End of Chapter Reflection and Questions

- **How will you share your foundational thinking of the BIST philosophy (mindset) with your grade level or building team?**
- **Discuss the six skills that will need to be taught and determine how to be more consistent.**
- **Complete Appendix 7.2 on your team/building.**
- **Review Appendix 7.3 and identify where you fall in the continuum. What support do you personally need? What can you do to support the growth of others?**

Appendix 7.1 Vision Team Considerations

- **Purpose**:
  - Guide building level implementation of BIST both philosophically and logistically
  - Create and maintain energy regarding the philosophy of BIST
  - Support building consistency
  - Assess strengths and obstacles of adults regarding philosophical balance of Grace and Accountability
  - Identify when specific concepts need to be revisited as a community
  - Create the vision to move from maintaining students to changing students
  - Support staff in planning for students
  - Build the foundation for ongoing conversations
- **Logistics**:
  - Meet a minimum of one time per month. Initially, may need to meet weekly or every other week.
  - Time frame should be limited to 30–45 minutes
  - Discussion is *always* focused on the adult community—not individual students
  - Group norms should be established
- **Team members should be**:
  - Selected by administrator in collaboration—voluntary participation can be included
  - A teacher leader who has a positive impact with the staff members
  - Passionate around supporting students who struggle
  - Representative of the entire faculty (a member from each team including encore/elective, or a member from each grade level including specials)
  - Vulnerable and open to learning
  - Has vision larger than their classroom
- **Facilitate meeting**:
  - Initially, administrator may lead to building capacity
  - As capacity is established, a teacher or counselor should facilitate meetings

- **Progression of implementation**:
  - First year: Vision team may spend time developing consistent forms for communication
  - Develops and communicates common language for staff, students, and parents
  - Implementation of BIST Continuum of Change
  - Members develop capacity to assist in planning for students
  - Continued assessment of philosophical foundation
  - Maintain inspiration and motivation for BIST vision
  - Ensure new teachers attend Basic BIST Training (accompanied by a current vision team member)
  - Ensure student plans are transferred from year to year
  - Analyze the strengths and obstacles in the building regarding BIST
  - Assist in setting up building level skill-based coaching
  - Create a calendar of reteaching regarding common area expectations, goals for life, skill-based coaching, outlasting continuum, processing, etc.
  - Analyze the data collected to ensure positive impact
- **Possibilities**:
  - Develop new student orientation ideas
  - Assist in the journey of equity for all students
  - Visit other schools to increase vision
  - Facilitate parent nights or parent classes
  - Attend BIST Vision Team Conference
  - Develop district-wide vision team networking opportunities

Appendix 7.2 Tipping Point Assessment

S = Success (90% of staff are proficient)
NI = Needs Improvement (65–89% of staff are proficient)
C = Concern (less than 65% of staff are proficient)

Concept	Rating	Comments
Foundational thinking (Grace and Accountability)		
Training		
Administration		
Teachers		
Support staff		
Common area structure		
Classroom management		
BIST Placement Continuum		
Data collection		
Prevention		
Building		
Classroom		
Individual		
Early intervention		
Gateway behaviors		
Caring confrontation		
Processing		
Planning for students		
Outlasting Continuum of Change		
Adult ability to collaborate in best interest of student		
Adult ability to address and support each other based on building commitments		

Appendix 7.3 Adult Continuum of Change

For leadership to increase staff capacity, they must become strategic and intentional.

Capacity: Increasing Ownership

Non-Compliance	Compliance	Partnership	Independence
• Struggles to follow through with stated staff expectations. • Is inconsistent with supervision assignments. • Creates a sense of distance among colleagues. • Intentionally or unintentionally undermines staff initiatives. • Has a fixed mindset regarding behavior and growth.	• Slower to embrace change. • Waits to see results of other colleagues during the change process. • Typically effective individually but may have limited impact with colleagues. • Can implement new information when directly supervised but may not be able to follow through consistently. • Is receptive to coaching, needs additional support for change.	• Participates in problem solving at both staff and student levels. • Willing to support leadership decisions. • Shares information to support other staff members. • Is able to take risks in order to grow professionally. • Is respectful in adult and student conversations. • Is receptive to coaching and can follow through with suggestions. • Has long-term goals for students beyond individual classrooms. • Able to mentor new staff members. • Able to assist other staff members in developing individual skills. • Plays an active role in leadership at the building level. • Supports other staff members with difficult students that are not in their classroom.	• Able to mentor new staff members. • Able to assist other staff members in developing individual skills. • Plays an active role in leadership at the building level. • Models appropriate problem-solving in staff settings. • Frequently leads problem solving with other staff members. • Addresses and supports colleagues. • Can articulate and implement vision for the school community. • Supports other staff members with difficult students that are not in their classroom. • Puts energy into implementation of initiatives. • Embraces change. • Explores concepts for new building growth.

References

Brown, Brené, 2012. *The power of vulnerability: Teachings on authenticity, connections & courage*. Louisville, CO: Sounds True.

Dolan, W. Patrick, 1994. *Restructuring our schools; A primer on systemic change*. Kansas City, MO: Systems and Organizations.

Gladwell, Malcolm, 2000. *Tipping point – How little things can make a big difference*. New York City, NY: Time Warner Book Group.

Sinek, Simon, 2009. *Start with why: how great leaders inspire everyone to take action*. London, UK: Penguin Group.

For Product Safety Concerns and Information please contact our EU representative GPSR@taylorandfrancis.com
Taylor & Francis Verlag GmbH, Kaufingerstraße 24, 80331 München, Germany